MORE PRAISE FOR *ABOUT FACE*

"Dan solves the mystery of effective advertising by heading towards the face. It is the face that contains all the sensory organs (nose, mouth, ears, and eyes), as he calls it the immediate barometer. He suggests 10 dexterous rules in his recipe."

Kamal Georges Darouni, author of *Advertising and Marketing Communication in the Middle East*, assistant professor (NDU) and CEO Infomarkets Int'l Advertising agency

"In About Face, *Dan Hill shows how to inject the virtue of emotion back into business – an essential skill if you want to master the very human art of engagement and dialog in a world transformed by social media."*

Charlene Li, author of *Open Leadership*, co-author of *Groundswell*

ABOUT FACE

ABOUT FACE

THE SECRETS OF EMOTIONALLY EFFECTIVE ADVERTISING

DAN HILL

KoganPage

LONDON PHILADELPHIA NEW DELHI

Publisher's note

Every possible effort has been made to ensure that the information contained in this book is accurate at the time of going to press, and the publishers and author cannot accept responsibility for any errors or omissions, however caused. No responsibility for loss or damage occasioned to any person acting, or refraining from action, as a result of the material in this publication can be accepted by the editor, the publisher or the author.

First published in Great Britain and the United States in 2010 by Kogan Page Limited

120 Pentonville Road	525 South 4th Street, #241	4737/23 Ansari Road
London N1 9JN	Philadelphia PA 19147	Daryaganj
United Kingdom	USA	New Delhi 110002
www.koganpage.com		India

© Dan Hill, 2010

The right of Dan Hill to be identified as the author of this work has been asserted by him in accordance with the Copyright, Designs and Patents Act 1988.

ISBN   978 0 7494 5757 0
E-ISBN   978 0 7494 5923 9

British Library Cataloguing-in-Publication Data

A CIP record for this book is available from the British Library.

Library of Congress Cataloging-in-Publication Data

Hill, Dan, 1959-
    About face : the secrets of emotionally effective advertising / Dan Hill.
        p. cm.
    Includes bibliographical references and index.
    ISBN 978-0-7494-5757-0 -- ISBN 978-0-7494-5923-9 (ebk) 1. Advertising--Psychological aspects. 2. Decision making--Psychological aspects. 3. Advertising--Research. 4. Emotions. I. Title.
    HF5822.H515 2010
    659.101'9--dc22

                                               2010013860

Typeset by Saxon Graphics Ltd, Derby
Printed and bound in India by Replika Press Pvt Ltd

Contents

Introduction   *1*

01 Get physical   **9**
Orientation   9
Billy Mays and the gift of the gab   9
The variables of voice   10
Seeing what you can't see   13
What has the most visual stopping power?   15
Going beyond sight and sound into additional media   18
Leveraging sensory contrasts   20
Creative templates that work well   23
Summary   24

02 Keep it simple   **27**
Orientation   27
How not to waste half your advertising   27
Engagement: what the financial stakes are   29
Advertising's secret emotional cancer: frustration   30
Overcoming frustration through simplicity   31
Rules for word play   38
Summary   42

03 Keep it close to home   **45**
Orientation   45
Easy does it: the advantages of leveraging what's familiar   45
The comfort zone: where the familiar is credible and easy
  to accept   47

Leveraging people's preference for comfort   50
Taking into account people's bias against what's foreign   52
Summary   54

04 Focus on faces   **55**
Orientation   55
Why faces are special: proof and four well-known reasons   55
Why faces are special: subtle factors highly relevant to
  advertising   57
From theory to practice: emotional responses to faces   61
True smiles versus social smiles: how heartfelt smiles differ
  from willed ones   62
The quest for authenticity   64
Criteria for casting appropriately and evaluating
  performance   65
Summary   69

05 Make it memorable   **71**
Orientation   71
Did you see it? Recall measures as a house of mirrors   71
Explaining the answers: the gap between recall and how
  ad retention works   73
Explaining the answers: why 'Truth' won and what it
  means for you   76
Three additional criteria for enhancing ad retention
  based on how memory works   79
How to avoid the risk of creating unbranded ads   83
Summary   85

06 Relevancy drives connection   **87**
Orientation   87
The categorical truth: never forget the WIIFM   87
Types of motivations: a serious case of wanting fun food   89
Being on-motivation is essential to effectiveness   92
Redefining industry categories as emotional markets   94
Relevancy created by identifying with the emotions
  involved   97
Relevancy created by identifying with a brand's
  personality type   100
Summary   102

07 Always sell hope   **103**
    Orientation   103
    Happiness, Inc.: leveraging the hope that springs eternal   103
    The interrelated dynamics of happiness and hope: an
        advertiser's checklist   107
    A critique of three examples of selling both hope and
        happiness   109
    Behavioural economics and the tension between hope
    and fear in advertising   112
    The missing factor in selling hope: be true to your word(s)   117
    Summary   119

08 Don't lead with price   **121**
    Orientation   121
    How leading with price can destroy a company's
        marketing strategy   122
    Problem 1: Lack of sustainability (surprise fades)   123
    Problem 2: Become numb to price (devaluing hope)   123
    Problem 3: Invites analysis (undercutting emotional
        engagement)   126
    Problem 4: Low-value perceptions (inviting contempt)   127
    Problem 5: A price focus distorts purchase choices
        (dissatisfaction results)   128
    Problem 6: Brand loyalty at risk (pride takes a hit)   130
    Problem 7: Brand integrity at risk (desperation detected)   131
    In contrast, three real solutions to economic hard times
        and price/value wars   132
    Summary   135

09 Mirror the target market's values   **137**
    Orientation   137
    Why empathy has become marketing's new touchstone   137
    The struggle to create authentic dialogues: welcome to
        executive blogging   140
    The battle of sexism: offensive gender portrayals   143
    The rise of a creative class outside the advertising
        agency structure   146
    Cause marketing: a way to neutralize critics and make
        new friends   149
    Summary   151

10 Believability sticks   **153**
    Orientation   153
    The battle between belief and pervasive scepticism   153
    Defining the types of advertising   157
    What type of advertising is most emotionally persuasive?   159
    Time for analysis: what are the implications of these
        various results?   161
    The two ends of the spectrum for creating persuasion   164
    Familiarity: what we know and like, we trust   166
    Fairness versus desire: fulfilling on practical needs or
        wants and dreams   166
    Fairness: why humility and specificity work wonders   167
    Desire: it's all about the three Ps of passion, pleasure
        and purpose   167
    Consistency: nobody's won over by fickle companies
        and mono-emotion actors   168
    Summary   169

    Afterword   *171*
    Notes   *175*
    Picture credits   *185*
    Index   *189*

Introduction

SCIENCE MEETS CREATIVITY

Twentieth-century marketing (may it rest in peace) was largely about being on-message, about getting talking points consistently right. Or at least that's how corporate clients tended to view things. Agencies went along to one degree or another. In contrast, 21st-century marketing will be very different. With ever-gathering force during the past two decades, breakthroughs in brain science have confirmed what we all instinctively know in our gut but often don't admit to in business: people are primarily emotional decision makers. This book is about how 21st-century marketing can realize success by being on-emotion, first and foremost. Being on-message remains a vital but secondary strategy, a way to plug in just enough 'facts' that the rational mind, searching to justify a choice, can find them in the marketing and, therefore, feel confident about the purchase.

What do I mean by being on-emotion? I mean creating the right emotions for a particular person, at the right time, and in the right way to fit the positioning of a given offer (whether it be a product, service or experience).

To illustrate my point, picture a 30-second TV spot in which pretty women in flouncy, colourful dresses are bouncing around to upbeat music. A diet drink is being advertised. So far, so good – until my company finishes testing it and discovers through scientifically reading the faces of the target market (middle-aged female consumers) that the most striking emotion in response to viewing this spot is sadness at three times our norm. Sadness? That's hardly the emotion the client was hoping for. So what's creating this result?

To understand the dynamics, I have my staff first isolate when exactly the reactions happen. As it turns out, most of the sadness was being felt while the tagline, 'Pump it up,' was on screen. Okay, mystery half-solved. The triggering element is known. But why is this happening, and why sadness? I have my staff comb back through the test subjects' verbal responses looking specifically for comments related to sadness, disappointment, buyer's regret.

Bingo. Knowing what needle in the haystack we're looking for enables us to find the problem and solution quickly. We discover that a significant minority of the women tested found the tagline too aspirational. Put simply, 'Pump it up' made it sound to the middle-aged women of the target market that the pretty women in colourful dresses depicted in the ad are workout fanatics, who go to the gym all day long just to get in shape. We learn that the thumping music, the tagline and the ever-so-slim and pretty women combined to make the target market feel sad instead of happy. In summary, 'Pump it up' came to symbolize a bridge too far to cross for the middle-aged women. Their conclusion? 'This diet drink offer isn't for me.' But that's only half the story.

What is the client's response to this analysis? They agree that the target market's reaction makes sense. In focus groups, this multinational company had heard some fuzzy comments about the 'Pump it up' tagline but until now had been unable to identify, much less quantify, the problem. We have done both.

Unfortunately, the company's solution is to simply tone down the thumping, gym-like music a bit and downplay the tagline by making it less prominent and moving it toward the end of the TV spot instead of interspersing it throughout the spot. Ideal? Probably not, but at least it reduces the threat of off-emotion advertising that could alienate the target market and reduce acceptance of the offer. A better solution would have been an on-emotion spot with an on-message, intellectual alibi that justifies the choice and reinforces confidence about the purchase.

Gauging emotions helps to connect with consumers

By degrees here, I'm trying to tell you what this book is about and what you, my reader, will get from it. Let me do so, first, by telling you the basis of my authority to write this book. I'm no genius, but I do enjoy the advantage of being a Marxist, or more precisely: a Groucho Marxist. I'll explain. In an old Marx Brothers movie, Groucho says to his stuffy dowager nemesis, Margaret Dumont, 'Who are you going to believe: me or your own eyes?' If you've been on earth for more than a few days, I think you'll agree with me that 'your own eyes' is a better way to go than traditional market research, which depends on verbal 'lip service' input.

People lie, consciously or unconsciously. But fortunately you will become privy to a natural, non-invasive (no sensors) way to figure out people's true emotional reactions. Then your company can market to consumers more effectively. This non-invasive system is called facial coding, and it consists of

The essence of 21st-century marketing: being on-emotion

Forget about whacking people over the head with canned messages. Being on-message reflects a fading broadcast business model imposed for years in print ads, over the airwaves and now, though faltering, with website pop-up ads few people notice. By comparison, feelings are natural, innate and organic to all of us. So being on-emotion defines the new marketing era, which champions 'pull' instead of 'push'.

reading people's emotions through how the muscles on their faces move in combination to reveal seven core emotions. Facial coding goes across cultures; even a person born blind reveals through their facial muscle movements their emotions in the same way you or I do. Given a 'wow' like that, it's no surprise that facial coding has entered popular culture through books like Malcolm Gladwell's *Blink* and a TV show like Fox's primetime hit, *Lie to Me*.

For over a decade now, my company, Sensory Logic, has used this unique research tool to get at how people feel their feelings, rather than think their feelings by answering survey questions. In *About Face: The Secrets of Emotionally Effective Marketing*, I will reveal to you specific, actionable take-aways that major, global blue-chip companies have paid large amounts of money to acquire. For the readers of this book, I have pulled together the key lessons – patterns, insights and secrets – that a wealth of case studies have revealed to me over the years.

Is there value in what I'm offering? I think so. The upheaval in the marketing realm is so great that columnist Bob Garfield of *Advertising Age* has described it as a profession that 'doesn't even know what it is any more'.[1] The Age of Interruption is over. The Digital Revolution, led by social media, is upon us, and amid all the technology, the gadgets, the new digital wiring, few of us know for sure what to do any more. I am here to reassure you that through measuring and managing emotions, there is, indeed, a way forward.

Let's begin by understanding how people make decisions, because, as you will come to understand, at the deepest, most profound level, creating an emotional connection *first* provides the solution. From engagement to brand loyalty, everything is feelings based. Think of this book as an advocate for combining the new digital wiring with some really old wiring. I'm talking about the human brain. But in truth I should be talking about human brains, plural, because we have three of them. As scientists have known for decades now, there's the original sensory (reptilian) brain, an emotional (mammalian) brain (both millions of years old) and finally, since some 100,000 years ago, a rational (human) brain, where our verbal abilities reside.

In business terms, this means that first-mover advantage rests overwhelmingly with the older, sensory–emotive way in which your marketing connects with consumers. Creating a strong sensory–emotive connection is at the heart of making money. In contrast, a rational, on-message approach is vital, but secondary in that it provides the intellectual alibi. By that I mean: give people a way to be interested (leveraging the sensory brain), a reason to care (leveraging the emotional brain), and then and only then a confirming reason to believe (leveraging the rational brain).

If you want a good return on investment for your marketing efforts, then you will profit from the specific examples and statistical patterns revealed in *About Face* because your strategy will change and reorient toward being on-emotion.

Two studies caught my attention before writing this book. The first appeared in 2008, touting a study from Omnicom Group that said managing to emotionally engage the target market really does move the sales figures. More specifically, the study found that engaging consumers resulted in a return on investment that's 15 to 20 per cent higher than if only mere awareness gets achieved.[2]

The 3.5-pound universe atop our neck

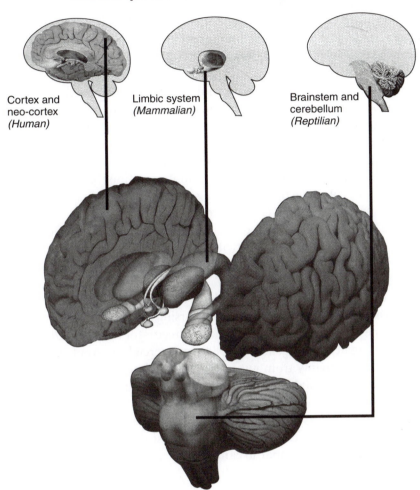

Cortex and
neo-cortex
(Human)

Limbic system
(Mammalian)

Brainstem and
cerebellum
(Reptilian)

Some Monday mornings you may feel like you have no brain at all. Rest assured: you've actually got three brains, of which the emotional brain is the key to success – because the value of the offer your company is promoting gets determined emotionally as an instinctive judgment.

Then, in early 2009, in an article titled 'Why emotional messages beat rational ones', Hamish Pringle and Peter Field reported that based on their review of 880 case studies from the UK's Institute of Practitioners in Advertising Effectiveness Awards, emotions win.[3]

More specifically, they found that 'soft sell' ads that inspire strong emotional responses in consumers make more money. In fact, they resulted in profit gains that were nearly twice as good as 'hard sell' ads with fact-based, rational arguments.

Furthermore, Pringle and Field also learned that campaigns that leverage emotions excel at reducing price sensitivity, are superior at creating a sense of brand differentiation, and become more important as a market sector matures.

Now, to fully establish the value and importance of being on-emotion, let's also look at marketing's woes. Yes, it's true that in a survey conducted by the American Association of Advertising Agencies, 69 per cent of my fellow citizens said they 'are interested in products and services that would help them skip or block marketing', with the result that 'industry executives are frantically searching for ways to forge more emotional connections' with consumers.[4] Yes, it's true that advertising is seen as a reliable source of information by fewer than 10 per cent of people.[5]

But the statistics that should really get your attention involve updates to the famous 19th-century quote attributed to both William Hesketh Lever and John Wannamaker. It's the one about how half of advertising gets wasted, but nobody knows which half.

More recently, the following experts have weighed in on the exact percentage of advertising effectiveness (or waste). Endorsing the low end of the spectrum of effectiveness is Lee Clow, global creative director for the TWBA/Chiat/Day agency that created the legendary '1984' commercial for Apple Computers. Speaking most probably from gut instincts in an interview that appeared in *Fast Company*, Clow said that one of the realities of advertising is that '90 per cent of the work has always been terrible'.[6]

Other estimates have tended to come from market researchers. John Hallward of Ipsos says that the company's vast database of results shows that under 50 per cent of global ad campaigns achieve their goals. In contrast, 20 per cent of global ad campaigns do have a significant impact on sales for their sponsors.[7]

Rex Briggs and Greg Stuart, co-authors of *What Sticks: Why Most Advertising Fails and How to Guarantee Yours Succeeds*, assert that of the nearly $300 billion spent on advertising annually in the United States alone, some 37 per cent of it is 'wasted'.[8]

Meanwhile, a decade before either of those sources, John Philip Jones weighed in with what is perhaps the single most definitive study. A total of 2,000 US households were involved, using meters attached to home television sets and a hand-held scanner to track the codes of products purchased. The study lasted over two years and involved 78 advertised brands. What was Jones's main conclusion? Some 30 per cent of the advertising studied worked pretty well, of which a third worked extremely well. Another 40 per cent worked less well. Finally, 30 per cent of the advertising was so bad that Jones found that sales actually declined as a result of its being on the air, with the big brands disproportionately suffering from the most mediocre advertising.[9]

In other words, only about 15 per cent of marketing works great. Another 40 per cent is a flop, or even counterproductive, giving you reason alone to keep reading this book to do better!

THE BOOK'S STRUCTURE AND CONTENT

Although I love Luke Sullivan's book on advertising, *Hey, Whipple, Squeeze This*, I'm simply too curious and persistent to entirely accept his verdict: 'Why most of it stinks remains a mystery.'[10] What follows in *About Face* is why it's no longer as much of a mystery to me. Using 10 rules to guide you, the book addresses the following key questions: how to create interest, from increasing your brand's stopping power to establishing a powerful brand personality; how you can lock in interest, enhancing recall and consideration; and finally, how you seal the deal, affirming the value and trust you'll need for your marketing to be persuasive.

These 10 rules are not what you might suspect, or fear. They're not commandments. Rather, this is a book dedicated to exploration. The 10 rules speak to human nature, which is infinitely complex. Writing her poetry in the mid 19th century, Emily Dickinson couldn't have known that the four inches between our ears hold about one hundred billion neurons. Still, she was correct in saying that 'The brain is wider than the sky.'

It's also, sadly, far wider than the perspective most companies take. I agree with Al and Laura Ries's critique that advertising's fundamental dilemma nowadays consists of being seen as 'one-sided, biased, selfish, and company-oriented rather than consumer-oriented'.[11] So to affirm the importance of dialogue and echo this famous statement from *The Cluetrain Manifesto* – 'Markets are conversations'[12] – I've secured the input of 20 people from around the world through professional international contacts and a friends-of-friends network.

Here (on page 8) are their names, faces and the countries they call home. You will be seeing excerpts from interviews with them appearing inside grey boxes, along with quotes in black boxes from marketing professionals.

As noted by Denise Shiffman, the author of *The Age of Engage*, in this new emerging era of advertising, 'hearts, not eyeballs, count'.[13] That's because from the use of the internet for website searches and forum posts, to podcasting, blogs and interactive ads on subway walls, the heart of the matter is now consumers' distributed *experience* as opposed to a company's marketing *message*.

The chapters that follow move beyond the old product-centric Ps of product, price, place and promotion, to three new people-centric Ps. That's because in advertising, feelings influence us three times over. First, there's our immediate, often subconscious reaction to an ad based on our sensory perceptions of it and real-time emotional response. That's the passion 'P'. Second, to be competitive, a company will give its offer more than functional meaning by linking it to the higher calling of the target market's emotionally-laden values and beliefs. That's the purpose 'P'. Third, a company whose brands come across as emotionally engaging, unique and authentic will have more character and be easier to identify with. That's the personality 'P'.

The bottom line takeaway, however, is simple. Emotions rule decision making. By focusing on passion, purpose and personality, your company's marketing campaigns can help you step closer to consumers and ahead of the competition.

1

Get physical

ORIENTATION

Using as many of our five senses as possible will create more effective advertising. The urgency of creating stopping power requires going beyond the common senses of sight and sound to invoking the other three senses when possible. We're not abstract thinkers. Great advertising is something that you see and hear, and today you might also smell, taste, and feel it.

Another reason to engage people across the sensory bandwidth is that the new generation of consumers, especially those at the cutting edge, where so much of the spending power is located, will reject being mere consumers. They want to be advertising's co-producers, people who condone or dismiss the messaging of companies based on how it is shaped and experienced by them, in their own bodies, through their own senses.

The pertinent emotion for this rule is *surprise*, the opportunity to stop us in our tracks and set up the opportunity for prolonged interest in the offer, as we encounter advertising executed in a way we might have never expected.

BILLY MAYS AND THE GIFT OF THE GAB

It's Billy and Barb, the dynamic duo. I've never seen my sister-in-law like this before. I'm standing in her spotless kitchen in suburban Chicago, watching her eyes narrow, then disappear, amid laughter so hearty that nothing – not her head-shaking, no; nor her 13-year-old son watching her eyes tear up over bathroom humour; nor the fact that we've watched this parody of a Billy Mays TV spot for the third time in a row – can bring a stop to her enjoyment. In that, Barb's not alone. The parody, called 'Billy Mays Big Piece of Shit Slider Station', is typical of both the straight-up and parody versions of his TV spots on YouTube. The number of viewings can reach as high as 200,000.

In fact, of the thousands of commercials that Barb has seen in life, only two really stand out: an ad from Coca-Cola, and anything starring the now recently deceased Mays. In Coke's case, it's 'That old Coke commercial,' where Barb 'saw people standing in a line, connecting the world. *Make the world sing…* nice. The people there: it just had, it just gave me a good feeling.'

But Billy Mays is different. When asked, 'What works at grabbing your attention?' Barb tells me, 'I hate to say it, but – loud noise. I'm thinking of Billy, the guy who does all those as-seen-on-TV [products]. It's obnoxious, but the minute I hear it, it's like, *That's him*. What grabs my attention isn't necessarily what keeps my attention. But I look because he's got a loud voice. He's got some new product worth 'Ten times its weight in water' or whatever. And in response,' concludes Barb with both a sigh and another huge, eyes-disappearing smile, 'I'm like, I've just *gotta* have it.'

Welcome to one of the key realities of connective advertising. It isn't always pretty, and it's rarely complicated. Often something as basic as responding to a voice (its volume, pitch and speed) can carry the day when it comes to the first key factor in advertising effectiveness: stopping power.

Notice I didn't say 'attention'. Stopping power is much more commercially valuable, because merely gaining attention isn't the same as knowing whether or not an ad grabs our attention and *stops* us in our tracks. Stopping power beats surface-level awareness as an advertising yardstick because it speaks to changing consumer behaviour.

Barb hears Billy Mays, turns to look at him – and wants to buy whatever the guy is selling. In other words, the sound of Billy's voice is also the sound of ka-ching, of money being made. Why? That's because in a world where the mind is geared to filtering stuff *out*, Billy Mays' loud voice proves to be the perfect set-up. His distinct personality helps him carry his message effectively. His TV spots aren't really geared to rationally oriented awareness (I recognize you). Instead, they embody emotionally oriented stopping power (I can't not listen, and look, and want your endless parade of $19.99 items that promise to solve a variety of nagging household problems).

THE VARIABLES OF VOICE

Billy's loud voice is his way in, the opportunity, part of a formula that from an auditory perspective works far better than anybody in advertising might expect, for several reasons. First, let's take *volume* into consideration. A good way to isolate that variable is to focus on radio spots. After all, while the essence of television is moving pictures, and the essence of the internet is interactivity, with radio its essence is the human voice on behalf of communicating with emotion and a vivid personality.[1]

We tested radio spots using facial coding to capture emotional response as a way to investigate whether talking at the top of your lungs, as happens in Billy Mays' TV spots, contributes to stopping power or not, based on captured emotional response.

Here's what Sensory Logic found from numerous radio spots in its database. People emoted more, over 24 per cent more, to louder radio spots. They also had, by 18 per cent, a higher impact (arousal) level in emotionally responding to louder spots. And amazingly, going loud didn't kill appeal (likeability). In fact, the average appeal score of loud spots was nearly twice that of moderately loud spots.

In short, loudness qualifies as attention grabbing. (For advertisers, that's a good thing since people's multi-tasking ways – online while 'watching' TV, for instance – mean that other media are now joining radio as a backdrop to whatever else they're doing.)

> *Sounds are good. I like little beats of electronic music. I do not pay attention to more of the serious ads with the serious voice.*
>
> Hugo Martin Feu, Argentina

Moving on from volume, *pitch* has two aspects to it. First, a lower pitch is generally considered better by voice experts. A deep voice suggests competence and credibility, whereas a high-pitched voice suggests nervousness and volatility. Second, in general the greater the amount of pitch variability the better, since it suggests energy and passion.[2] In Billy Mays' TV spots, we've got a guy with a low – though not particularly low – pitch, accompanied by a limited variety in pitch.

A third factor is speed or *tempo*. In general, slightly faster is considered better because people who speak more quickly often get perceived as more competent, persuasive, as well as more likeable. Research indicates that people who speak about 20 per cent faster than average have more influence.[3] On average, the typical English-language speaker says 125 to 150 words a minute, but will most likely be able to comprehend words spoken at twice that speed.

In Billy Mays' case, over the four TV spots that we checked, he spoke at 182 words a minute. That's 21 per cent over the normal range but well within the limits of what viewers can follow.

Beyond volume, pitch and speed, what else might influence the effectiveness of vocals used in advertising? One consideration is whether to allow for flaws and quirks. For instance, should 'ums' and 'ahs' be included in the sound track?

I don't tend to pay much attention to information that is forced on me. Sense of humour is very important. With the French, if something makes you laugh, then you are more inclined to like the product.

Jean-Charles David, France

In Billy Mays' case, the 'ums' and 'ahs' have been edited out. Fine, in the TV spots he's not giving a speech. But so, too, are the pauses – perhaps leaving money on the table. Our radio database shows that about 10 per cent of all the emotional response occurs during the slight pauses that are typically left in during the delivery of a script. Why such a relatively large amount of emoting during dead-air time? The answer is that variation helps to avoid monotony. Furthermore, pausing may enhance curiosity as well as create clarity and opportunities for key words or phrases to be emphasized, register and sink in.

Finally, there's another aspect that's relevant here. Both sounds in general, and voices in particular, have associations that come with them.

In a study conducted in a wine store, the shelves were stocked with four types of French and German wines otherwise identical in price and dryness or sweetness. Then either French or German music was played on alternative days over a two-week period. When French music played, 76 per cent of the sales went to the French wines. When the German music played, 73 per cent of the sales went to the German wines. Among the shoppers who agreed to answer a questionnaire during the two-week test period, however, less than 15 per cent of them said 'yes' when asked, 'Did the type of music playing influence your choice of wine?'[4]

So, what does that wine study have to do with loud-mouthed Billy Mays? My hypothesis is that the late Billy Mays' high-energy voice, apparent conviction and, to quote my sister-in-law Barb, hopelessly 'serious' manner are all on-emotion. In this case, it isn't fine wine that's being sold; instead, it's solutions to those nagging problems that plague you. Billy Mays takes your seemingly trivial problems seriously when nobody else will.

SEEING WHAT YOU CAN'T SEE

In Florence, Italy, on market day I once saw a table loaded down with Jesus Jeans. The product's tagline was 'The ultimate designer'. Provocative, yes, but unpublicized. I never saw them advertised on TV. That distinction belongs to Calvin Klein jeans, whose 1980 campaign featured a languid 15-year-old Brooke Shields asking the audience, 'You know what comes between me and my Calvins? Nothing.'

Questioned about the scandal that ensued – CBS and ABC stations banned the TV spot – Calvin Klein blandly voiced surprise, saying he didn't believe anybody could 'read' anything into his 'things of beauty'.

Soon to follow was Brooke Shields purring into the camera: 'I've got seven Calvins in my closet. If any one of them could talk, I'd be ruined.'[5] Surely, 'reading' these spots wasn't the key to their notoriety and success, nor the reason why Calvin Klein recently authorized a billboard in New York City showing a teenage girl in a threesome (with suggestions of a foursome).

The average American can read 250–300 words per minute. In contrast, visual input takes everybody on the planet only about two milliseconds (ie two-thousandths of a second) to reach the older, sensory–emotive parts of

Decades later, the original Calvin Klein ads featuring Brooke Shields still make an impact. This girl does her best imitation of a pose that Shields made famous.

the brain. That same visual input then takes 250 times longer to be consciously recognized by the newer, rational brain. Clearly, from an evolutionary, survival basis, we process visuals much more efficiently than we do the copy that might appear in ads.[6] In this case, the speed with which we comprehend visuals is a huge benefit. Everybody understands the Calvin Klein jeans campaigns *instantly*.

How big an advantage is visual accessibility? Consider the fact that the global literacy rate is 82 per cent, which sounds pretty good, unless you are going to advertise in India, for instance, where the literacy rate stands at 61 per cent. Moreover, two-thirds of the world's 771 million illiterate adults are women, often the primary shoppers.[7]

Another advantage of on-emotion visuals is that you bypass language barriers. In today's global economy, don't let a foreign tongue stand in the way of stopping power. In the United States, for instance, about 20 per cent of people speak a language other than English at home. By the year 2050 the world's diverse marketplace is projected to consist of 1,384 million native speakers of Chinese, 556 million of Hindi and Urdu, and 508 million of English. Spanish and Arabic will clock in at 482 and 468 million speakers respectively.[8]

Now, none of this is meant to suggest that a words-based or words-only piece of advertising can't be fantastic. For instance, an ad for Mercedes–Benz consists of blurry words like 'road', 'traffic' and 'sidewalk'. The one word that stands out clearly is 'child', placed dead centre to promote a new brakes system that can read the road, thereby protecting a young pedestrian and the driver alike.

Is it the exception that proves the rule, however? I think so. Two numbers tell the story. The first is the cliché that a picture is worth 10,000 words, whereas written language is estimated as coming into existence a mere 5,000 years ago.

In summary, my point is similar to what Luke Sullivan wrote in *Hey Whipple, Squeeze This*: 'Find one great image and build a story around it.'[9] That's what Calvin Klein's agency did with the Brooke Shields campaign, and you could say that a lot of primal instincts came alive.

Whatever leaves an impression on my mind is what I gravitate towards and look for in the stores. I like an advertisement that is very subtle but makes a huge statement and has longevity, a history and a legacy.

Jennifer Jenkins, Colorado, United States

Cave drawings are but one tangible sign of the primacy of visuals. Such imagery is still compelling, centuries later. Three of the seven secrets of eye tracking are hinted at here, given how the drawing focuses on implied, sudden or ongoing motion.

WHAT HAS THE MOST VISUAL STOPPING POWER?

Besides facial coding, eye tracking results can also help provide an answer. When I started Sensory Logic over a decade ago, I wanted to monitor gaze activity. But it wasn't until the Swedish company Tobii came along that I felt eye tracking was viable because previous systems had been too cumbersome and invasive.

Using technology based on five cameras built into a screen that looks like a large, desktop computer monitor, the stage is set for capturing split-second readings of where people gaze most and longest, on average. More results will be shared in Chapter 2. But here are eye tracking's seven secrets: five guidelines for what draws the eye in still images (print ads, outdoor, web pages, direct-mail envelopes), followed by two additional guidelines for moving imagery.

Five guidelines for still imagery

1. Down the centre. Put the most important image front and centre. We like to get oriented, which is energy efficient and makes us feel emotionally comfortable. This placement makes sense because we process visual information far better when it is in the middle of our field of vision rather than on the periphery. Something that's in the centre gets looked at by both eyes, each covering for the other eye's blind spot.

   Example: A Miller Beer print ad attracted attention dead centre, where the beer bottle nestles up against an empty, waiting glass.

2. Faces. As will be discussed in depth as Chapter 4, faces draw attention readily and constantly. The combination of this and guideline 1 will capture most gaze activity.

3. (Implied) Motion. Other body parts can attract attention, too. Yes, cleavage draws attention but that's not my main point here. It's that an outstretched hand, for instance, or a person jumping in the air and caught freeze-framed draws our attention. Our 'visual system is exquisitely tuned

to biological motion'[10] because, in general, stationary objects don't signify either attacks or food, ie the risks or rewards that are central to surviving and thriving on the planet from an evolutionary perspective.

Example: A General Mills cereal advertising campaign in which the leaping lady is delighted by the prospect of improving her health by eating well.

4. What's meaningful. We long for meaning and are constantly searching to buttress our lives with meaning and purpose. In regards to stopping power, that translates into risks and rewards.

    Example: A Kraft ad for Seattle's Best means that, of course, despite its small size and placement in the lower right corner, all eyes gravitate quickly to the cup of coffee situated there.

5. What's dominant. The larger the size of something, generally the more important we consider it to be. A day with a key meeting is a 'big' day. The eye goes to what is proportionally dominant, or in other cases more brightly lit, more colourful and so on.

Let me also say a few words about words here. As shown by eye-tracking results, most people skim-read. A few words early or late in the copy may get attention. The rest? Barely. Increased font size helps; using an unusual font type can help, too. A single word placed next to an object or used in combination with any of the five guidelines above is your best chance for getting noticed.

Two guidelines for moving imagery (video)

1. Sustained action. 'Down the centre' and 'Faces' aside, movement arrests the eye and constitutes stopping power. Sometimes that's true even when faces are present.

    Example: A Bud Light Lime commercial was shot *cinéma vérité*-style, not literally black and white but so muted in colour as to be nearly so, with a faux hand-held-camera quality to the footage. The commercial itself shows a faceless Lime as it dances and tosses coasters, winning almost all the attention (with the exception of the coasters themselves, which are flying around the room, too). Despite the other people at the party, less than 5 per cent of the gaze activity lands on them.

2. Sudden movement. Everything else on screen can be fairly static, creating the opportunity for attention to be seized by the introduction, movement or disappearance of an object, person or even a part of the script.

    Example: In a Rosetta Stone spot, a sentence pops up in the middle of the screen once the spot's primary narrative is over. However, the sentence has a gap in the middle – where a series of words flashes, drawing the eye. The words that flash into the gap are 'extra', 'enjoyable' and 'interacts', giving the company a trio of visual pay-offs.

GOING BEYOND SIGHT AND SOUND INTO ADDITIONAL MEDIA

In our media-soaked world, every form of promotion needs an opportunity to be noticed. So beyond the use of sight (and sound) in TV spots, use of the other three senses of touch, taste and smell can, must and will increase in marketing in general. That's true because media like event marketing, outdoor and in-store can be experienced in a way that can engage all five of our senses, thereby achieving a greater connection than is possible with traditional media exposure.

> *More creative is now in designing where the advert is going to go, rather than the message creation. Live events engage people, immersing them in the product experience. The contrived doesn't stand a chance in the same way.*
>
> Paul Springer, author/consultant

Bringing promotions alive

Quiksilver's ability to co-opt skateboarders into riding right over their logo feeds into teenage rebellion. It also causes the skateboarders to inevitably and repeatedly notice the branding effort.

How big is the opportunity? Our senses take in an estimated 400,000,000 bytes of information per second.[11] As shown here, we're all sensory logicians because, within the brain, each of our senses has its own special territory to handle each specific sensory signal. Failure to engage every sense lets brain real estate go to waste, undermining the opportunity for your ads to break through the clutter.

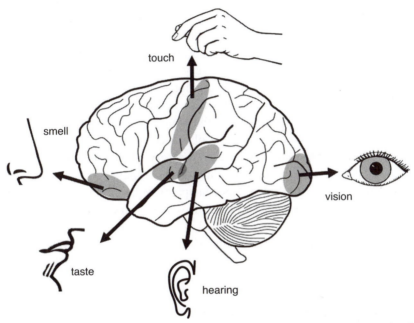

Different parts of the brain have their own sensory speciality. We think of the cortex as devoted to rational, abstract thought. But in fact the vast majority of the cortex is used for sensory processing, with only the frontal lobes reserved for non-sensual tasks.

Now let's focus on the three senses not normally highlighted in advertising, for the simple reason that their marketing potential is so vast.

Smell. One study found a 40 per cent improvement in people's mood when exposed to pleasant fragrances. Another study found us willing to pay over $10 more for shoes displayed in a scented as opposed to unscented showroom. Only about 3 per cent of the companies that belong to the Fortune 1,000 have a distinct scent for their different brands.[12]

Example: To dramatize the dangers of carbon monoxide, my friend Joe Rich at the utility company PSE&G created a scratch-and-sniff mailer to point out that an odourless substance can kill you without any sensory warning.

Touch. Skin serves as the body's largest organ. Touch allows us to thrive. Indeed, 'Massaged babies gain weight as much as 50 per cent faster than unmassaged babies. They're more active, alert, and responsive...and are emotionally more in control.'[13] Likewise, as adults, sensitivity to touch remains a key part of life.

Example: In Malaysia, Sony advertised its PlayStation® 2 with bus-stop signage that incorporated the texture of bubblewrap to invite people to touch it. The idea was that the bubblewrap's raised Xs and Os suggest the tactile quality of the PlayStation's controller, inviting people to explore the bubble-wrap in anticipation of then getting to play with the PlayStation itself.

Taste. While people have 10,000 taste buds, this sense will probably be more difficult for advertising to leverage very often. That's because of health concerns related to tasting and/or ingesting something new, especially if we don't personally interact with a representative from the company offering it.

Not to be deterred, Adnan Aziz, the founder of First Flavor, Inc., has arguably created the first advertising tool to incorporate taste. Inspired by the 1971 film *Willy Wonka and the Chocolate Factory*, in which Gene Wilder plays Willy and lets kids sample the fruit-flavoured wallpaper in his surreal candy factory, Aziz dreamed up Peel 'n' Taste Strips. Whether appearing in mailboxes or magazines, the strips serve as an alternative to grocery-store sample stations, capturing the flavour of almost any food in a tiny package.[14]

Should you think that leveraging *all* of the senses in advertising isn't worth the bother, think again. For example, consider what Sensory Logic's database reveals. In cases where we've tested products where a certain sense was dominant (eg perfumes, for smell), we've found that the smell, taste and touch of a product create an engagement level that's three to four times higher than the engagement level stimulated by merely seeing the product being displayed.

LEVERAGING SENSORY CONTRASTS

Across cultures, there are certain sensory contrasts that we often collectively take for granted, and might not consciously notice, but we still use them as ways to intuitively understand the world around us. Examples of these contrasts include: big versus small, hard versus soft, and relaxed versus tense. Built into each of these contrasts is the collective weight of associations that companies can exploit to ensure that their marketing campaigns have greater immediate meaning and persuasive impact.

Let me point to the single most prominent example I know of that takes advantage of these contrasts. It's the ad campaign ranked number one of all time in *Ad Age*'s listing of the top 100 advertising campaigns. I'm talking about the 'Think Small' campaign created by Doyle Dane Bernbach in 1959 for Volkswagen. At that time in car history, big was unquestionably accepted as better. In introducing the VW bug, instead of glossing over the size issue (the bug clearly was not big) the campaign flaunted the small size of the Volkswagen Beetle. Thus the VW's smallness became a virtue, with the offer positioned as the far more clever David battling the giant Goliath that was then true of General Motors both in terms of the size of the cars it was manufacturing and its market share in the car industry.

Today, we are accustomed to ever-smaller cellphones and other electronic gadgetry and we often think of smaller as better, more nimble, compact and energy efficient. So in retrospect it might be hard to recognize the revolutionary nature of this ad.

What normally happens in a car ad, even to this day? The car is front and centre, prominent, larger than life. In 'Think Small' (page 22), the car occupies perhaps 5 per cent of the visual field, a further exaggeration of its small size. In its heyday, the VW Beetle was a huge anomaly. Acknowledged as a 'little flivver' in the ad copy, the Beetle was such a break from the big mindset of Detroit's US-made cars that as late as 1978, almost 20 years later, General Motors was building a Cadillac Eldorado that was 18.6 feet long and weighed 4,906 pounds. With an engine compartment that's been described as a '425-cubic-inch beast', the Eldorado was 'riotously big' and epitomized the conspicuous-consumption mindset – big is better, big is power and might – that the 'Think Small' campaign was lampooning.[15]

In short, 'Think Small' effectively used the sensory contrast of big versus small, and effectively altered the then-prevailing bias towards one in favour of a smaller size. Moreover, it did so decades ahead of Seth Godin's *Small Is the New Big*.[16]

Deep down, sensory contrasts work because the oldest, sensory brain is a pattern-matching machine. The natural world around us provides many sensory contrasts that companies, if smart, can leverage for their own gain, strategically choosing to exploit one side of the contrast or another to convey the essence of their offer or, in the case of Burger King, leverage both sides of a single contrast in different decades. I'm referring here to the sensory contrast of relaxed–tense.

What has Burger King done? Back in the 1970s when being 'mellow' was in style, the company's famous 'Have It Your Way' tagline championed being relaxed. Seeking to differentiate itself from McDonald's, Burger King sought to tap into the mood of the country by implying that its bigger rival served up standard fare in a rush-rush manner, indifferent to what customers really wanted.

Think small.

Our little car isn't so much of a novelty any more.

A couple of dozen college kids don't try to squeeze inside it.

The guy at the gas station doesn't ask where the gas goes.

Nobody even stares at our shape.

In fact, some people who drive our little flivver don't even think 32 miles to the gallon is going any great guns.

Or using five pints of oil instead of five quarts.

Or never needing anti-freeze.

Or racking up 40,000 miles on a set of tires.

That's because once you get used to some of our economies, you don't even think about them any more.

Except when you squeeze into a small parking spot. Or renew your small insurance. Or pay a small repair bill. Or trade in your old VW for a new one.

Think it over.

Long before the Arab oil embargo of 1973 made the United States think again about its love affair with big cars, VW struck with this great ad, heralding the virtues of small.

More recently, however, Burger King has taken the opposite side of the contrast. On behalf of pitching itself to its key demographic of young men more likely to be into extreme sports these days rather than wearing earth shoes, Burger King's advertising has become edgy, tense, featuring a King who is anything but mellow. While Ronald McDonald is a do-gooder, the King is mischievous.

As the two examples of the VW Beetle and Burger King show, sensory contrasts bring together properties of the natural world within the context of the era in which an offer is being positioned. Tangible and universal in nature, sensory contrasts provide a way of implicitly framing a campaign in terms that give it greater meaning than it would have on its own. Not to take advantage of these contrasts is to be as blind to the physical properties of the world, as if all companies were to choose grey as their corporate colour.

CREATIVE TEMPLATES THAT WORK WELL

Finally, no discussion about creating stopping power would be complete without a look at the six sensory-oriented creative templates that a team of Israeli scientists discovered in studying award-winning advertising.[17] While many of us may have wondered about whether there are patterns to the type of creative work that possesses stopping power and works well, here's the rigorous process the Israeli team followed.

First, award-winning ads and contest finalists of New York's The One Show and also the *USADREVIEW* were assembled for the years spanning 1990–5. Of these, 500 ads were randomly chosen and provided to a trio of 'creative experts' with at least a dozen years of experience in the advertising field. These experts privately chose what they considered to be the highest-quality ads from the 500, resulting in 90 per cent agreement about what were the best ads.

Next, discussions resolved the remaining choices in order to arrive at the 200 best ads. Given the set, the Israeli team began studying the 200 ads. Their eventual conclusion: 89 per cent of the ads could be described as belonging to one of six creativity templates, with pictorial analogies accounting for over a third of all the best ads. In brief, here's an overview of each template, including a top-line description of an ad that illustrates the template.

Pictorial analogy. Portrays situations in which a symbol enters the product space. An example of an extreme analogy rendered visually would be a Nike ad that adopts the perspective of somebody leaping from a tall building. What will cushion the fall? Down on the street a group of firemen are holding an oversized Nike sneaker. The tagline reads, 'Something soft between you and the pavement'.

Consequences. Shows the implications of either following or ignoring the recommendation made in the ad. An example is of eggs sizzling in the 1980s commercial, 'This is your brain on drugs.'

Extreme situation. Depicts unrealistic situations that showcase the importance of key attributes of a product or service. An example is an ad for a security lock whose value is demonstrated by showing a woman, her voice replaced by that of a dog, barking at burglars to scare them away.

Competition. Shows situations in which the product competes with another product or event from a different class, such as a race between an advertised car and a bullet.

Dimensionality alteration. Distorts or otherwise manipulates the physical dimensions of the product in relation to its environment. For example, in a life-insurance commercial a wife is arguing with her husband for cancelling his policy. The catch here is that the scene is taking place after he's died, and the wife is communicating with him through a séance.

Interactive experiment. Inspires a realization of the product's benefits by requiring the viewer to engage in an interactive experience. An example is that Café Crown created door hangers with samples for college students nearing exam time, giving them a chance to experience their coffee at a time when stress levels were high and the students would have maximum appreciation of coffee that keeps them awake and stimulates their thoughts.

To finish the Israeli research team's story, consider this. In a subsequent review of advertising that didn't win awards, they found that only 2.5 per cent of the ads fitted one of the six templates. Who would have ever thought that creativity was so rote! Of course, it isn't – but that's not the point here. The point in regards to stopping power is that the six creativity templates often grab our attention and stop us in our tracks through the use of the unexpected portrayed in tangible, physical terms. Novelty surprises us, and has great impact: in terms of facial expressions; surprise causes the eyes to go wide and the mouth to fall open, as if the body is telling us: look around, pay attention, stop talking.

SUMMARY

As we've seen throughout this chapter, the bland status quo is the enemy of stopping power. More and strikingly unique sensory stimulation equals more mental activity. Vision is the only sense that we have the ability to turn off. So to be on-emotion by creating surprise and enabling connectivity, the entire sensory bandwidth should be up for grabs. Going from two-dimensional to five-dimensional advertising will be one hallmark of the future.

Takeaways include:

● Stopping power is more commercially valuable because merely gaining attention isn't the same as knowing if an ad grabs our attention and *stops* us in our tracks.

- There are seven eye-tracking secrets, including: centrality, dominance, showing faces, and showing or implying motion.
- Beyond the use of sight and sound in TV spots, use of the other three senses will increase because experiential media like event marketing, outdoor and in-store are so conducive to leveraging more than sight and sound in order to overcome media clutter.
- Leveraging sensory contrasts enables companies to frame their campaigns in terms of physical associations that carry great intuitive meaning.
- Eighty-nine per cent of award-winning ads fit one of six creativity templates, involving depictions that seize on or distort the physical properties of the world as we know it in order to highlight an offer's value.

2

Keep it simple

ORIENTATION

The advertising goal at stake in this chapter is engagement. Stopping power's a start. In retail terms, that's like tempting the shopper to enter the store and stand at the threshold. But if any money's going to be made, the shopper has to go deeper into the store – in the same way that engagement involves creating substantial, often prolonged, emotional interest in an ad. What most often keeps that from happening? Needless complexity leading to frustration. After all, what doesn't come easily typically doesn't come at all: frustrated consumers will choose to disengage. Therefore an overly large degree of complexity in advertising is toxic.

Put another way, the joke that has to be explained to you is *never* as funny as the joke that you just get. So it is in advertising. The Keep It Simple (Stupid) KISS principle is relevant here because the cause of frustration is feeling like things are out of your control, including whatever advertising you're experienced that has left you confused.

HOW NOT TO WASTE HALF YOUR ADVERTISING

In my Introduction, I mentioned the famous quote that haunts advertising: 'Half my advertising is wasted, but I don't know which half.' Well, what if you *did* know and could avoid the waste? Quite frankly, as the following example illustrates, facial coding makes that possible by pinpointing when, in *real time*, consumers are engaged or disengaged by advertising.

At Sensory Logic, the key way we measure engagement is to quantify the number of test participants who, in response to exposure to an ad or discussing it, show an emotional response that we can quantify scientifically. So if, say, 10 people out of 50 reveal at least one codeable response, then that represents a 20 per cent engagement level. In cases where we have exposure that unfolds over time, as is the case with TV and radio spots, there's also the distribution of second-by-second *feeling points* to consider. We plot feeling points in real time. Look at these results from a 60-second radio spot.

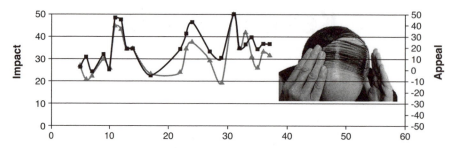

For the first 38 seconds, this spot is cruising along great. Then listeners drop out, bored by the voice-over, hence the image of a man's bald spot. For the last 22 seconds of this radio spot, nothing, nada: emotionally empty real estate.

What's the darker line here? It's the appeal score, which is the number of positive feelings generated relative to negative feelings. A higher level means more appeal. What's the lighter line here? It's the impact score or the intensity or strength of the emotional responses. There are many ways the appeal and impact scores can interact, but in general the higher the scores the better, even though higher scores are not always the most important story.

In this case the important story is about the number of feeling points and their distribution over time. In this case the key is the *bald spot* that appears after second 38.

What's going on? The first 38 seconds of this spot work well because of the drama involving the characters in the ad: Loser Dude, Cool Dude and a hapless female folk singer in a club somewhere. Both of the guys want to leave. She's awful. But Loser Dude can't leave. He's paid for the club's WiFi. In contrast, Cool Dude has got mobility – thanks to the sponsor's laptop WiFi connect cards.

Up to second 38, this spot is very engaging and is also *on-emotion* (appeal falls when Loser Dude speaks, and rises when Cool Dude speaks). So what happens after second 38? There's commercial death, a bald spot, a duration of exposure where there aren't any feeling points. So the coy answer would be that absolutely nothing happens. But here's the real explanation. Just prior to second 38, the radio spot switches gear and Loser and Cool Dude disappear, along with Dreadful Folk Singer. After second 38 the spot is dominated by the professional voice-over talent that comes in to sell the branded offer more explicitly.

There's nothing wrong (technically) with this female voice-over. It's smooth. It's polished. It's clear. It's articulate. But it's an emotional *void*. There's no sense of passion or conviction or authenticity to the Voice-Over Lady.

Moreover, the Voice-Over Lady sounds generic, like a million other such voice-overs. So it's no surprise that listeners – as indicated by the bald spot – will go away. In short, the sponsoring company paid for 60 seconds of advertising, but got only 38 seconds of value. Ouch!

ENGAGEMENT: WHAT THE FINANCIAL STAKES ARE

Engagement matters; in fact, it's tremendously important. With it, exposure brings gain. But without engagement, there's no sustained interest, little opportunity for retention and almost certainly no opportunity for consideration or persuasion. The example I just shared makes that point.

But maybe like Cool Dude, you're a born sceptic. You say to yourself: prove to me that engagement matters in financial terms.

Here's validation based on an instance where the Gallup Organization joined up with a research firm in San Diego to benchmark customers' engagement levels regarding a Japanese luxury retailer. In this case, fMRI brain scans were used to monitor blood flow in the brain while people answered simple yes–no statements about the retailer. In the end, what stood out from the testing is that the highly engaged test subjects (those whose brains were most active), proved to be the same people who spent the most money in that particular retailer.[1]

As Gallup affirmed, engagement might be thought of as stopping power turned into sustained attention, interest and commitment. Like the brain, faces feed us subconscious information. What we know as happiness, surprise, anger, fear, sadness, disgust and contempt are like the primary colours of red, yellow and blue. They're building blocks that we experience intuitively.

These primary emotions aren't soft 'touchy-feely' things like traditional business theory would have us believe. Instead, they're vital to survival and, if anything, even more vital to marketing because 'Advertising does not first get attention, and then create an emotion. Advertising creates an emotion, which results in attention.'[2]

As a result, engagement and emotions alike are at the heart of advertising effectiveness. To learn what works, we've reviewed our database of TV and radio spots to offer a top-line summary of what typically causes emotional momentum (hot spots) or disengagement (bald spots). Across those two media, here are some guidelines to help you ensure that your money's well spent.

In TV spots, famous faces, slow motion and zoom-ins work best. With radio spots, the use of dialogue, pauses and punchlines engages people the most. Meanwhile, in both media the greatest danger consists of monotonous voice-overs, which kill momentum. That's no surprise. As stated in Ambrose Bierce's *The Devil's Dictionary*,[3] the definition of a bore is 'somebody who talks when you want them to listen'.

ADVERTISING'S SECRET EMOTIONAL CANCER: FRUSTRATION

As important as emotional engagement is as a barometer of creating – or losing – the chance to connect with your target market through advertising, there's another barometer, too: it's *frustration*. During a decade of market research tests that, thanks to facial coding, enable me to study consumers' real-time responses emotion by emotion, I've found that (unfortunately) frustration is the number-one negative emotion felt by us in response to exposure to advertising.

> *When an ad tries to tell you everything in words in such a short time, it can be very frustrating. I do not think regular viewers follow so many words.*
>
> Momoko Kang, South Korea

The table opposite shows the overall levels, in rounded numbers, by marketing medium. Note that they're ranked high to low in terms of the amount of frustration created.

The good news here – slight as it is – is that with the exception of the top two examples, television animatics and website exposure/navigation, the amount of *happiness* (smiles) also being shown by consumers at this time exceeds their levels of frustration. But the bad news remains: we experience lots of frustration, ie anger, when we encounter the nine different types of marketing listed in the table opposite.

Most of us would agree that Apple CEO Steve Jobs is a pretty savvy marketer and he advocates 'elegant simplicity'. The research of Rex Briggs and Greg Stuart has led them to the conclusion that the ads that work best are, almost without exception, 'straightforward'.[4]

Moreover, a study reported in Gerd Gigerenzer's book *Gut Feelings: The Intelligence of the Unconscious* shows that baseball players do far better when they don't over-think their decisions on the playing field. That's because gut instincts are nature's way of improving our odds of survival – a skill that overly complex ads undermine.[5]

Frustration Caused	
TV Spots (animatics)	40%
Web (exposure/navigation)	38%
TV Spots (storyboards)	34%
Product Usage	32%
Sales Scripts	29%
Radio Spots	29%
TV Spots (fully produced)	28%
Print Ads	26%
Packaging (exposure and/or opening of)	24%

Why so much frustration? Two factors, I believe. First, people are rushed, distracted, tired, uninformed – you name it. They just don't have enough mental resources left to get it. Second, those with all the financial resources in the world – companies and their ad agencies – make the connections too readily. They suffer from the tunnel vision of failing to recognize either the surfeit of information (the company's fault) or pacing that overwhelms people, burying engagement (the agency's fault); and everyone suffers.

In *Ogilvy on Advertising*, David Ogilvy cites a study that found that of 25 'typical' television commercials being analysed, *all* of them were miscomprehended by 19 to 40 per cent of the people involved. Ogilvy's conclusion and subsequent admission? 'If you want to avoid your television commercials being misunderstood, you had better make them *crystal clear*. I cannot understand more than half the commercials I see.'[6]

Now, just a note about the table above: yes, the testing of unfinished TV spots (ie animatics) can frustrate people, for instance, because they're so accustomed to polished TV spots. That said, however, the average level of frustration in response to fully produced TV spots, radio spots and print ads is, on average, nearly 28 per cent. Moreover, the typical website experience is plagued by frustration that comes in at 38 per cent.

Dissatisfaction. Discouragement. Disengagement. Those are hardly the goal of marketing. So let's discuss causes – and solutions.

OVERCOMING FRUSTRATION THROUGH SIMPLICITY

There's no money in making people feel stupid. We don't look favourably on a company for making us work too hard to follow along. Instead, we just give up and go away. Or as the populist politician George Wallace once reportedly said: 'You've got to pitch the hay where the goats are' (and they're rarely on the mountain top).

I'll start with visual guidelines – rules for the eyes. After all, images register ahead of the printed or even spoken word.

Choose accessibility over obscurity

To build on the eye-tracking guidelines I gave you in Chapter 1, let's begin with the need for quick comprehension as the first rule for the eyes. Since the brain takes about half a second to react to a stimulus,[7] if nothing happens that quickly, then consumers' first emotional response is a void.

To make my point, here's an example. Even more than other forms of marketing, billboards have to be accessible, given the speed of your car and all the distractions (like other cars) that are, frankly, more important than taking in a billboard. Seems obvious enough, right? Nevertheless, that reality wasn't enough to keep a major packaged goods company and its agency from developing a billboard that had two fatal flaws.

For the company, the first problem was that the cereal's colouring blended right in – so aesthetically harmonious but oh, so invisible to the eye against the amber background of the billboard. The eye literally couldn't pick up the cereal's distinct shape, on display, piece by piece, interspersed between a series of black Xs.

Nor did the second problem help matters. Down below the row of cereal pieces sat the phrase, 'The 1 and only'. However, the digit 1 was so close to the word 'and' that many people read it as 'land', making them read the caption as 'the land only' – creating utter confusion. Now back up to the typical situation, where people are driving and they see, not the cereal, but the black Xs and then 'the land only' if they even get to the text.

Well, that's a commercial disaster. It's hard for the product to be the hero if the product is invisible. What's physically obscure or blurry runs the risk that it will create an equally blurry emotional response in all of us.

> *Sometimes it is so complicated and confusing. It is really hard to concentrate on watching television if the ads are very fast.*
>
> Jalal, Qatar

Provide perspective: create a path through the woods

As a general rule of thumb, we prefer global information (the forest) before getting local information (the trees). Essentially, what this means is that we want to see the whole picture first, before the parts. It's a matter of getting us oriented to a new situation, and comfortable, thanks to what's simple and easy.

Therefore, a company and its agency can create a stronger emotional connection with us if they'll provide the big picture first, and do it visually. In scientific terms, here's why. The sensory and emotional brains occupy more of the right and rear side of our craniums. The rational brain sits more on the left and front side of our craniums. It's the emotionally-oriented right hemisphere that processes in a holistic – big picture – fashion and is oriented to spatial relationships. In contrast, our left brain processes in piecemeal, detail-oriented analytic fashion, and favours what unfolds over time.

Right–left brain specialization also means the brain's two hemispheres get crossed. As a result, the right brain reacts first – but in doing so it draws on sensory data from the left eye and ear. Does that mean that having your visual on the left side of a still image and your copy on the right side will create a stronger emotional response? Brain science would suggest so.

But consider the typical home page layout in a website, for instance. The standard is to have a left-column navigation layout. Moreover, that's not the only potential issue involved when it comes to designing a website that will work from both a usability standpoint and aesthetically in order to, on the one hand, avoid frustration; and on the other hand, inspire engagement.

Someone keen on achieving both functional usability and aesthetic pleasure is web developer Jason Beaird, whose article, 'The principles of beautiful web design,'[8] provides five major guidelines to ensure optimal web design. Here they are, followed by our survey of 10 consumer-oriented websites from among the ranks of companies listed in the top 25 by *Fortune*:

- Content before design. The design should facilitate scanning the page for the information we want. A good design leads the eye without getting in the way of the page's readability or organization.
- Intuitive navigation. The primary navigation block should be clearly visible, and each link should come with a descriptive title. Items should be easy to find, thanks to being separated visually from the content.
- Unity. A cohesive, coherent theme or style should unify the pages of a site, with repetition a key device. Two approaches aid with this goal: proximity, ie placing objects close together to create focal points; and the repetition of bringing similar items together.
- Visual balance. Balance is crucial. Symmetry is one way to handle this need, but asymmetrical balance can also be achieved by arranging objects so that they visually equalize despite varying weights.
- Emphasis. Specific elements should draw our attention. The isolation and contrast of key elements are two ways to achieve this goal. Working with proportions, or differences in the scale of objects, is another means to that goal.

Does this all seem too nit-picking? Hardly. First, remember that after TV animatics, website exposure and navigation are the second greatest source of marketing-related frustration. *Grrr.*

Second, here's my review of the 10 websites. Despite a wealth of financial resources, most of the companies struggle to adhere to Beaird's guidelines.

Top 25 FORTUNE Companies (Consumer Websites)							
Fortune 500 Rank	Site	Rating (0-5)	Content Before Design	Intuitive Navigation	Unity	Visual Balance	Emphasis
2	Walmart	4	x	x	x		x
6	General Motors	4		x	x	x	x
7	Ford	4		x	x	x	x
8	AT&T	3	x	x			x
11	Bank of America	3	x	x			x
14	IBM	5	x	x	x	x	x
17	Verizon	4	x	x	x		x
19	CVS	3		x	x		x
24	Costco	1			x		
25	Home Depot	5	x	x	x	x	x
			70%	90%	80%	40%	90%

Maybe money can't buy you love; it certainly can't buy you the perfect website. Using five criteria from a website guru, Sensory Logic conducted an internet-experience audit. How easy and pleasing was it to be on these sites? The good-news results speak for themselves. In contrast, visual balance was often a problem because companies stick to a single colour or limited palette – failing to draw on how different colours can serve as visual guides, lending emphasis and separation.

Provide a clear hierarchy of visuals

In Chapter 1, I wrote about the sensory-leveraging value of having a dominant visual. That point is built into Beaird's criteria, too. It's important to design based on what detail will be the single most arresting visual detail, then the second most arresting, and on downward from there, in a clear hierarchy of significance.

Visual clutter is nobody's friend. Connectivity suffers. For one thing, as Luke Sullivan writes in *Hey, Whipple, Squeeze This*: 'Every element you add to a layout reduces the importance of all the other elements.'[9]

So imagine my chagrin when Sensory Logic was asked to test some direct-mail pieces for a major insurance company in which their attempt to sell to *everybody* meant they seemingly showed most everybody in every single piece. The greater the number of people in a photo spread, generally speaking, the less positive consumers' emotional response to it. In this case, a mailer whose cover image showed only five people netted a 52 per cent positive score. In contrast, a mailer with nearly a dozen people on the outside cover netted an emotional result of only 35 per cent positive feelings.

To show that there were far too many people on the cover of the direct-mail piece to take in easily – or to emotionally care about – I brought to the presentation a final PowerPoint® slide showing Leonardo da Vinci's 'Last Supper'. My point here (besides interjecting a little humour) was to indicate that at least in da Vinci's case the eye knows where to look. There sits Jesus, clearly the focus of attention thanks not only to sitting in the middle of the gathering but also, of course, because of the golden halo around his head.

News flash: da Vinci's better than a direct-mail layout artist

What's the easiest thing for the recipient of a direct-mail piece to do? Decide not to decide (into the trash can it goes). Don't make that default option any easier for us than it already is. In companies, the consensus decision-making style makes it natural to think 'Let's add one more thing. More is better.' But in reality, filler is harmful because it doesn't help direct the viewer.

Don't put your logo in the corner of death

In comparison with stopping power, engagement happens over time. But the longer duration doesn't mean it goes on forever. Far from it. The average time spent looking at a print ad is less than two seconds.

A European study involving 1,300 print ads and 3,600 participants found the average to be exactly 1.7 seconds: with 0.6 seconds devoted to imagery, 0.7 seconds devoted to text, and 0.4 seconds to noticing a company's logo. Moreover, in testing across the three elements of brand, imagery and text, here's what that study also found. When logo size goes up, text attention loses out more than the imagery. When text size increases, the imagery suffers. But when the imagery expands in size, the other two elements are only marginally harmed, making prominent imagery the best way to go.[10]

Meanwhile, another study provides guidance on the typical pattern that the eye travels in absorbing a home-page layout (time duration not specified). Notice the pattern.[11]

The path the eye typically takes

Here's proof positive that knowing how people behave can make your marketing efforts much more effective. A branded offer can make you money, an unbranded design surely won't. In other words, your logo in the lower right corner typically gets seen too late in the visual-scanning process.

Proof negative: One time I was meeting with a hotshot web designer. In response to my suggesting that eye tracking and facial coding could tell him where consumers look and how they feel about his designs, the guy replied: 'Why would I want to know that?' As they say in court, I rest my case.

Much like the way in which people shop, the eye lands first slightly in from the left side. Similarly, shoppers typically go a couple of steps into an aisle before turning to face the merchandise, get oriented, and decide what specifically to focus on.

Once you have the advantage of being able to use eye tracking to gauge reliably, behaviourally, precisely, what people look at, when, for how long and in what order, you would most likely be amazed at just how often there's no good flow to a layout design. What does 'good' flow mean? There are two aspects to it. One is aesthetic, inviting us visually into the layout in a way that will create the chance for a sensory–emotive connection, ie engagement.

The second protects commercial viability, which brings me to the addition of a skull-and-bones emblem in the lower right corner.

Most disturbing for the companies who sponsor advertising – and want it to be effective by promoting not general sales but, more specifically, sales of *their branded offers* – is that the identity of the sponsor often goes unnoticed. I refer to the lower right-hand corner as the corner of death. That's because as the pathway chart shows, it's the second-to-last place we look. That's right: second to last when you've got only 1.7 seconds to connect. And yet it's the *first place* agencies put their clients' logos for all ad executions except TV spots, as we found from checking out advertising examples from projects that we've done in recent years.

Logo placement by percentage

Overall Results

8%	1%	10%
2%	25%	2%
4%	6%	42%

Primary Placement by Medium

	TV: 88%	
		Print: 56% Billboards: 60% Direct Mail: 36%

See a problem? I do. Having just shown you that the lower right corner is the corner of death, lo and (fail) to behold, that's where agencies put their clients' logos most often in all but TV executions.

Give the viewer a chance to keep up with you

When it comes to editing video for TV spots, there's an extra consideration. The eye typically needs six frames, or one-fifth of a second, to move from one part of the visual field to another. Edit the video more tightly than that and two bad things happen. First, the gaze of consumers won't travel fast enough to shift from an image in one part of their visual field to another, causing the new image not to be noticed much if at all before the video moves on. Second, overly abrupt, tight editing – involving scene shifts that the viewer can't follow easily – raises the frustration level.

Unfortunately, this rule gets violated all the time. Let me give you two quick examples, both involving a major packaged goods company headquartered in Europe, so that you can see why this last rule for the eye is so important.

In the first example, a TV spot aired in Turkey worked great and was generally on-emotion. The product was a deodorant, and the people we tested felt sadness when the attractive woman with body odour wasn't being noticed by the man she fancies, and happiness when they finally exchange warm glances. The one off-emotion hitch was when the story shifted from the woman's home back to the office building's elevator, where she meets the man again. The scene shift happens too abruptly, creating frustration in viewers, and marring a span of over 12 seconds during which viewers have predominantly enjoyed the TV spot's storyline.

The second example from this same company involves a 15-second TV spot, which ends by transitioning from showing two actors on screen to a product shot. Clearly, the company wanted people to notice the product. But because the actors' faces are on the far left side of the screen, while the product is slightly to the right side, the eye-tracking results revealed that at first viewers keep looking at the place on screen where the actors' faces had just been. They didn't transfer their gaze over to the product quickly enough to take it in before text was introduced on screen, distracting viewers away from the product on display.

There, as in so many cases, it's good to remember that people process images better that are shown in the same visual field as before. In other words, there must be a reason to vary the location of images. Otherwise, leave well enough alone, because excessive variety undercuts effectiveness.

RULES FOR WORD PLAY

The degree to which we're visual creatures as opposed to wordsmiths can hardly be overstated. While William Shakespeare used some 29,000 words in writing his plays and poems, the average American has a vocabulary of only about

8,000 words[12] or 28 per cent of Shakespeare's total. By and large, advertising is a seduction, not a debate, as affirmed by John Philip Jones's conclusion: more successful campaigns are neither hard-selling nor didactic in nature.[13]

Nevertheless, along with visuals there must be some guidelines for how to make copy work best to create emotional sparks. Here are the essentials.

Choose words that trigger simple pain–gain contrasts

A study conducted by Yale University came up with the 12 most persuasive words in the English language.[14] Here's the list:

1. You
2. Money
3. Save
4. New
5. Results
6. Easy
7. Health
8. Safety
9. Love
10. Discovery
11. Proven
12. Guarantee

What's striking about this list? To me, it's about how basic and emotionally charged these words are. Underlying the majority of them are really, after all, two other words: fear and self-defence – which makes sense because our survival instinct comes first.

Let me explain. Look at the list again and you'll see what I mean. What's the contrast to 'health' and 'safety'? It's vulnerability: illness and danger. What's the implied opposite of 'results', 'proven' and guarantee?' It's that you didn't realize any gain from buying something. In a similar vein, 'money' and 'save' can actually be interpreted as concerns about foolish spending, about wanting a gain, but fearing the experience, the pain, of realizing your money has been spent, but to no avail.

As a result, at least seven of the top 12 words are defensively oriented. Throw in 'easy' as a way of defending yourself against expending energy on something that's hard to do, and you can put fully two-thirds of this list into the category of self-defence. That leaves four words, of which 'new' and 'discovery' are about the allure of making a change, and 'love' and 'you' (as in me, the buyer) are about the thrill of finding somebody or some product/ service offer you cherish.

Put another way, the first rule of word play is not to get too conceptually grandiose. Looking out for number one, the individual consumer you're marketing to, remains a smart strategy.

Avoid elaborate claims (message-itis)

Related to the conclusion above is the second rule of word play: 'you' is more powerful than the offer's features. Far too many companies are egocentric, thinking in terms of themselves instead of 'you' the customer. As a result, they also see the offer as the hero and get caught up in what I call message-itis: marketing that's stuffed full of more messages, or claims, than consumers have the time, energy or intellect to absorb, or any interest in doing so.

Of all the speakers I've ever heard at a business conference, my favourite has been the guy at an Outdoor Advertising Association of America event in Palm Beach, Florida. There, in describing how hard it is to get clients to simplify their messaging – limiting themselves to a single main idea – he stopped to play a snippet from a song. His choice? 'One' by Three Dog Night to dramatize his point that, in advertising 'one' is, indeed, 'the loneliest number'.

> *If a lot of information about the product is being tried to be transferred to me in a 10-second commercial, it gets confusing. They'd rather consider putting only the main points of the product in it, the points that will really attract potential customers to buy the product.*
>
> Jan-Paul Wiringa, Holland

Too bad. For this book, I asked my staff to review our project files to count up the number of features, attributes and/or benefits mentioned per ad. Then we put the total up against the emotional-engagement percentage and the frustration level, as captured through facial coding. What we found is that ads with only one to three claims were 11 per cent more engaging and created four per cent less frustration than ads with four to nine claims in them. In short, less is often truly more.

For example, in testing a pharmaceutical sales script among doctors in Europe we found that the emotional response to the last third of the script was entirely negative because the participants felt, rightly, that everything being said had already been covered earlier. The repetition wasn't reinforcing; instead it was both dull and rather insulting to the doctors' intellects. Meanwhile, the most complex TV spot we have ever tested may have been a healthcare spot in which 86 words flashed across the screen in 30 seconds, along with 11 spoken words – far more than the maximum of 60 to 70 written words that John Philip Jones's research has found to be people's limit.[15] The result? Surprise, frustration and fear reactions at levels all far above norm.

That outcome confirms a statement made by the Heath brothers in *Made to Stick*, namely that 'Once we know something, we find it hard to imagine what it was like not to know it.'[16] They call this predicament the curse of knowledge. It's a curse that plagues chief marketing officers and their staffs, given the huge information imbalance between what they know and what we either know *or care to know*.

Focusing on a core idea is vital. Browbeating us with reasons why we should buy doesn't work. For those seeking to reduce message bloat, remember:

- Message-itis reflects an undue emphasis on the offer, neglecting consumers. For every feature/attribute you want to promote, ask yourself how you'd answer the question: 'So what?' Address benefits, *emotional* benefits.
- The more you get told, the less you know. As Herbert Simon has said, 'A wealth of information creates a poverty of attention.'[17] Faced with lots of claims, the rational brain simplifies anyway. As a result, emotions become decisive – subconsciously focusing us on what's most important and excluding the rest. Get there first and save people the effort by engaging in simplification yourself.
- Here are words to live by: 'Advertising isn't brain surgery. You want people who feel X about your product to feel Y. That's about it. We're talking one adjective here. Most of the time, we're talking about going into a customer's brain and tacking one adjective onto a client's brand. That's all.'[18]

Don't go for big words

One of the great things about direct marketing, maybe the greatest thing, is that you have a response mechanism to know what's working or not. So somebody who knows is Ben Suarez. Operating out of Canton, Ohio, Suarez has, over a 30-plus-year career in direct marketing, created a company that long ago established itself as more profitable than 99.5 per cent of all businesses in the United States.[19]

What has Suarez learned that relates to keep it simple? At least two things: 1) two pictures increase sales, while more than three pictures – or no pictures – lowers sales; 2) short words, sentences and paragraphs lift sales, while long sentences and big words or technical terms lower them.

That sounds simple enough, and wise. After all, in that list of the top 12 most persuasive words in the English language, five are only a single syllable and another five are two syllables long. Only one is three syllables, and only one four syllables, none is a bigger, longer word than that. But in terms of avoiding big words, how often is that rule actually adhered to in advertising? To find out, I asked my staff to compare print ads and direct mails from two sectors of the economy: automotive, and household products. Per sector, we reviewed 20 ads to determine how often the words used qualified as either complex or simple.

> *I find the most effective adverts can be the cheapest, tackiest kind.*
> *For example, radio adverts that constantly repeat the company name*
> *and contact details.*
>
> Tony Hodgson, England

Our definition of complex was that more than 5 per cent of the words in a given ad involved four or more syllables. By that measure, the household products category was in fine shape. None of the 20 examples we reviewed was stuffed with complex words. Simplicity ruled. But when it came to the automotive sector, suddenly 30 per cent of the examples qualified as mostly complex.

Maybe the idea is that to sell expensive products you can't use humble, 'nickel' words. Or it's a matter of positioning, since VW (the people's car) always fell into the simple category. But Peugeot and Fiat aren't more upscale than Mercedes–Benz, and yet they favoured more big words. You should know that your marketing is in trouble when just about the shortest word in your ad is a term like 'turbocharging'!

SUMMARY

Think too much, and you don't feel enough. Consumers who don't get emotionally engaged by your advertising out of boredom, or frustration, represent a lost opportunity. If leveraging the sensory bandwidth is the gate in the wall, then keep it simple is the opportunity to pass through the gate, en route to creating persuasion and sales. Ads that are too complex get lost in their own heads.

Takeaways include:

● Engagement involves creating substantial, often prolonged, emotional interest in an ad. What most often keeps engagement from happening is needless complexity leading to frustration.

- Engagement is like stopping power turned into sustained interest. That's because 'Advertising does not first get attention, and then create an emotion. Advertising creates an emotion, which results in attention.'
- Famous faces, movement and climaxes engage people. In contrast, monotonous voice-overs kill momentum.
- Additional rules for the eyes include: provide perspective, orient people quickly and easily, create a clear hierarchy of visuals and don't put the brand logo in the lower right-hand corner of death.
- Five visual guides for optimal web design consist of: content before design; intuitive navigation; unity of style; visual balance; and emphasis.
- To make copy work best, exploit pain–gain contrasts, avoid message-itis, and don't inflate your vocabulary level. Remember that the more we get told, the less we know, as the subconscious focuses on what's most important and excludes the rest.

3

Keep it close to home

ORIENTATION

The focus here is on generating likeability and preference through familiarity. The operative emotion is assurance; the operative term is comfort. In marketing, what's unfamiliar tends to get screened out by us. Go too far afield and you lose people. A far better approach is to use an existing zone of comfort to ease our natural fear of change. Most of this chapter will focus on that advice. But in closing I'll shift to addressing security, where fear of what's foreign affects how marketing works.

EASY DOES IT:
THE ADVANTAGES OF LEVERAGING WHAT'S FAMILIAR

Psychologist William Wundt, a contemporary of Sigmund Freud, created what is nowadays known as Wundt's Curve. It's his diagnosis of what it takes to communicate effectively. Besides being simple and novel, the other winning combination is complex and *familiar*. It's the inherent strength of playing to what's familiar in our lives that gives marketing enough freedom, or margin of error, to explore what's complex without becoming obscure.

There are two essential reasons why familiarity works. The first is *greater ease*, because what's familiar is more immediately accessible. For instance, research indicates that we instinctively recognize a familiar word like 'mother' in a mere one-tenth of a second. That's three times the speed of processing a less familiar word like 'ostrich'.[1] Two-tenths of a second may not sound like much of an advantage. But given that the average print ad only gets 1.7

seconds of attention, or that two-tenths of a second equals six frames of video in a TV spot, extra speed can be decisive.

Put another way, what's familiar gets absorbed readily because it doesn't require as much mental effort. That's why when Land Rover decided to become the first major brand to execute a national Twitter campaign, the company felt it could rely on hurriedly experienced venues like billboards and taxi TVs to seed so-called hashtags (words used in tweets that make it easier to follow an ongoing conversation via online searches). For those in the know, ie familiar with hashtags, fleeting exposure to the hashtags might be all that's required to help get a social media buzz going among Twitter users. Or so Land Rover hopes.[2]

Meanwhile, the other reason familiarity works so well in regard to accessibility is that there's then a *lack of filtering*. On average, we tend to screen out the unfamiliar, which requires more effort. Often the rational brain's prefrontal cortex filters information to reduce cognitive load. As a result, our feelings, always on – even if only subconsciously – automatically strive to analyse the world around us and 'capture the wisdom of experience'.[3]

> *Things that are not familiar don't mean that they are interesting. However, if something is familiar to me, I will keep watching it unless it contains a lot of wrong information.*
>
> Sadaaki Takata, Japan

For instance, in TV spots that Sensory Logic has tested we've often seen a surge in both emotional engagement and positive feelings when something very familiar comes on screen, even if the treatment itself isn't that special.

How strong is this bias towards what's familiar? So strong that if kicks and squirms can be taken as proof of acceptance, then babies in utero already prefer to have their moms repeat familiar stories aloud rather than experiment with something the yet-to-be-born child hasn't heard before.[4]

No wonder then that as a result of this familiarity bias the brain likes to follow a standard narrative formula: beginning, middle and suitable ending. It's an insight highly relevant to advertising, since abbreviated storytelling is one of its fundamental tools. A case in point is an ad for National Car Rental that shows a guy with his head down, having fallen asleep at the conference table while the boss drones on. The headline of the print ad is 'Get to boring meetings quicker,' which everyone in business can relate to. After all, who hasn't been in a meeting that was like a story with a beginning, a very, very *looooong* middle, but no plot – certainly no climax – just a merciful conclusion?

Meanwhile, in a different vein, for its new Fiesta, Ford is also trying to leverage the power of (social media) storytelling in hopes of creating familiar tales.[5]

In Ford's case, the idea is to simulate a 100-person test drive. By that I mean 100 'Fiesta agents' were chosen from some 4,000 online applicants to receive the car for six months in exchange for agreeing to post blogs about their experiences with the car. As Ford's Fiesta product manager, Sam de La Garza, was quoted as saying: 'We're going to allow people to tell the story [of the Fiesta] from their lives.' Whether Ford's social media initiative will work or not, who knows. But one story angle has already gained traction. Many of the people chosen to get the cars for six months for free have already been interviewed by regional newspapers or TV stations, based on their acceptance into the Fiesta Movement programme.

In summary, what's already known and readily recognized has a leg up when it comes to likeability. Our Keep It Simple brain prefers to function like a probability computer, looking to predict what is likely to happen next based on what it already knows.

> *Familiar details that I have seen effectively used in ads are working people who are always rushing and do not have time for themselves. Anything that is not familiar will be totally ignored as it is a waste of time to listen to it.*
>
> Kadulliah Ghazali, Malaysia

The fact that most easy-does-it assimilation happens on a subconscious level doesn't matter. In fact, if anything it's most likely helpful to advertising because the lack of conscious contemplation lowers the risk of objections being raised. Surprised? Don't be. As psychologist Robert Zajonc wryly observes: 'People generally prefer things they have seen before, even if they do not remember seeing them.'[6]

THE COMFORT ZONE: WHERE THE FAMILIAR IS CREDIBLE AND EASY TO ACCEPT

Besides providing easy accessibility, the other major positive reason why it's best to keep it close to home is that familiarity increases acceptance. Advertising is more emotionally connective, and effective, when its contents have already been internalized as part of us. That's because the brain rewires itself to accommodate the influence of previous experiences. As a result, when presented with what we already know, we enter a feedback loop, or memory echo chamber, which makes us ever more mentally and emotionally invested in what's familiar to us.

Home is where the heartbreak is

Think your marriage is tough going? Try being a Cubs fan. It's been like forever since the team last won baseball's World Series. This ad for a home-town company leverages the heartaches of Cubs fans in Chicago and elsewhere, working to create a warm, fuzzy, nostalgic feeling for the image as well as for the company itself.

For advertisers, this feedback-loop phenomenon represents a bonanza. Persuasion depends on our acceptance of claims explicitly or implicitly made about the offer. Well, due to the feedback-loop phenomenon, 'The brain unconsciously assumes that familiar information is true information.'[7] So how can agencies and their corporate clients trigger this same familiar-is-true-and-hence-acceptable formula? Scientific and psychological research would indicate the following.

Repetition. A path to fabricating familiarity is to repeat something until it becomes well known, thus subconsciously accepted and believable. Taglines are meant to work this way. Allstate can say, 'You're in good hands.' And if Ford says 'Quality is Job 1' often enough, the odds of our believing it go up. Moreover, a claim reiterated suggests it's important and worthy of remembrance, a mental signpost that may help to steer a purchase decision some day down the road.

Casting. The simple fact is that we relate best to others with whom we share looks, a similar vocabulary, and even a similar name. One study found that when sent surveys by mail, people were nearly twice as likely to complete and return the survey (56 per cent to 30 per cent) if the survey came from somebody with a similar name to the recipient. (When asked later, none of the test participants thought this factor had influenced their behaviour.) Want a testimonial that hits home? Get a person as similar to your target market as possible.

> *I'm tired of looking at white women in commercials. They do not represent all of us. I would love to see different-looking women. So I really like the Dove commercials because there are natural, big and curvy women in them. I like the different shapes of the bodies. If something is reproduced and fake, then I do not like it.*
>
> Jennifer Jenkins, United States

Soundtrack. Along with visuals and other sound effects, music isn't just a production choice; it's a potentially very meaningful, emotional signifier. Everybody knows that music induces feelings. It's also obvious that whether you're a rock fan, or a country, folk, bluegrass, jazz, rap or classical-music lover, among other options, your musical taste says a lot about who you are and may even signal where you come from. So choosing just the right genre of music and even specific artists to suit the target market is a natural.

What's less obvious is why 'canned', mechanized soundtracks are a staple of both TV and radio spots. After all, our research finds that generic soundtracks generate far less of an emotional response than do identifiable songs. When a canned soundtrack plays it generates feeling points only 13 per cent of the time: that makes it one-fourth as engaging as when identifiable music is playing. Moreover, when the known music is playing in a radio spot, the percentage of positive emotions felt by people is 23 per cent higher.

In summary, companies and their ad agencies are always talking about getting closer to consumers. Along those same lines, in *The Little Blue Book of Advertising* the authors even say: 'Know your audience is the single most important tip in this book.'[8] But *to truly know* how it feels to be that audience. *To truly know* what differentiates the target market from a rival's core customers. That's hard to do unless those who advertise take 'keep it close to home' seriously as a rule, and go beyond demographic data in order to empathize with those they seek to persuade.

> *Tell powerful existing customer stories. Then you are operating from a place of truth, which is the highest place to be. We have so much reality television going on, I would actually like to see a little more reality advertising.*
>
> Denny Post, CMO, T-Mobile

LEVERAGING PEOPLE'S PREFERENCE FOR COMFORT

How important is it to build a brand, through advertising, that we see as sharing our perspectives and attitudes? How strong is the tendency to be attracted to what reminds us of ourselves?

Like Unilever's famous and often loved Dove ads, an ad like this depicting average people helps us connect more readily and see ourselves using the product. For everyone, from young girls to older women, who don't get to see themselves portrayed much in advertising at all, let alone positively, ads like this represent a very positive step.

Based on the global research conducted by Ipsos, the answer to both the above questions is 'a lot'. The more a brand matches its target market, the greater the rise in purchase intent.

In fact, when the number of personal associations linking a brand and the target market is at its maximum level, Ipsos found that the linkage actually drives purchase intent scores 15 per cent higher than does even an equally optimal match between a brand and the target market's aspirations.[9] In other words, our comfort zones come first. In contrast, when fear becomes the operative emotion it's often because the familiarity that facilitates accessibility, promotes likeability and supports acceptance now either disappears or feels under attack.

As Leslie Hart says in *How the Brain Works*:

> *Under threat, we… run, fight, seek the comfort of a group, or the security of home or a substitute shelter… Commonly, we also temporarily lose the power of speech – one of the newest brain functions – and at best can make only some kind of noise… [We resort] to more traditional, more familiar, cruder behavior – to what we would do if we had much less brain.[10]*

Reducing our affective response to near zero is hardly what companies should be striving for. And yet that's what they too often inadvertently do by reducing our comfort level. What's the flip side of acknowledging that people accept what's familiar as true? It's when a company goes against the grain of what its target market has internalized, with the result that its advertising dies a quick death.

Much of Al Ries and Jack Trout's landmark book, *Positioning: The Battle for Your Mind*, is devoted to this very topic. What doesn't reinforce our sense of home and security, destroys it. Here are a few highly relevant passages:[11]

> *In general, the mind accepts only that which matches prior knowledge or experience.*

> *The mind has no room for what's new and different unless it's related to the old.*

> *The basic approach of positioning is not to create something new and different. But to manipulate what's already up there in the mind. To retie the connections that already exist.*

Or most of all:

> *Once a mind is made up, it's almost impossible to change it… The average person can tolerate being told something which he or she knows nothing about. (Which is why 'news' is an effective advertising approach.) But the average person cannot tolerate being told he or she is wrong. Mind-changing is the road to advertising disaster.*

In other words, we see what we expect and hope to see. 'Keep it close to home' is vital because we have a strong tendency to shut down and ignore, avoid or otherwise suppress noticing anything that goes against our preferred way of seeing things (eg listen again to Kurt Cobain singing 'a denial, a denial, a denial' at the end of Nirvana's song, 'Smells Like Teen Spirit').

Want your marketing efforts to be filtered out? Carelessly demolishing the target market's collective comfort zone will do the trick. As a result, in advertising it's a matter of promising something new, but not too new.

TAKING INTO ACCOUNT PEOPLE'S BIAS AGAINST WHAT'S FOREIGN

Deep down, acute sensitivity to what's foreign or otherwise new and different involves protecting our own beliefs, our familiar perspective on life. Nothing could be more intimate, closer to home, than our memories and innate expectations. So when we feel under attack, it's natural that we seek to identify, and blame, an outside force. What's foreign to us becomes the potential threat.

Over the years, at Sensory Logic we've seen how three otherwise all but identical home-mortgage print ads created very different degrees of positive emotional appeal – depending on whether the families shown were Caucasian, African-American or Asian-American.

We've also seen how a print-ad campaign for a US-based pharmaceutical company was responded to very differently in different markets. Options with African-Americans in them did fine in Europe, for example, but then they fluctuated in performance in America, depending on test locale. Meanwhile, the image of two female South Korean doctors did far better in Japan than elsewhere. Despite historical animosity between the two countries, it was a case, based on race, of *my tribe,* thereby creating appeal. (The other 11 ads were all, crazily enough, missing Asians despite the stated goal of launching a global campaign).

Yes, those might be extreme cases. But discomfort with strangers remains endemic to human nature.

It does have to be designed for me and I also have to relate to it through characters/actors who are nice, with a friendly attitude. As long as there are pleasant, friendly people, then that is the familiarity I relate to.

Jean-Charles David, France

A global campaign that mistook Asia for being practically empty

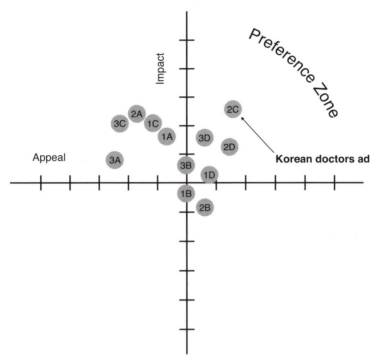

Does Asia constitute one-twelfth of the world's market? Hardly. But in testing in Japan, we found that, deprived of other similar faces, participants gravitated to those of their fellow Asians. There was nothing notable about the photograph otherwise. In *The Sopranos*, they might say: 'My people will talk to your people.' But in real life, opposite camps rarely do talk.

Clearly, we–they empathy has its limits among at least some people. But there are also cases in which the label of being foreign simply leads to an emotional void. It's as if there's no internal map by which to relate to those we don't know (well). By map, I sometimes mean that literally. Geographic illiteracy among young Americans is so pronounced that, in a test, only 37 per cent of them could find Iraq on a world map in 2006 – despite the fact that US troops had by then been in the country in highly publicized combat for three years.[12]

Almost as shocking to me was the lack of emotional reaction to a gorgeously filmed TV spot that we tested for a company in the automotive sector. The spot in question showed first a Russian family, then an Asian family, then an African family, to make the point that squabbling, impatient kids is a problem all parents, everywhere, struggle with. It was a good spot, I thought. But maybe since only 34 per cent of all Americans own a passport (compared with 41 per cent of Canadians, for instance),[13] the spot came in last emotionally among six spots because it involved places my fellow Americans haven't visited and don't know much about.

In short, it would be nice to believe everyone can empathize with everyone else in the world, and relate to those in faraway places. But it's more likely that, quite often, out of sight isn't just out of mind but, sadly, out of heart, too.

SUMMARY

The benefits to advertising of keeping it close to home consist of a target market enjoying easier recognition, enhanced comfort and a greater sense of security. Those are hardly trivial table stakes. Stated in negative terms, advertising that doesn't provide what's emotionally familiar runs a greater risk of failing to resonate. Think of Apple, for instance. That brand cult is built on a sense of uniqueness and a celebration of self-actualization. The perceived stranger is Microsoft, which the loyal followers of Apple couldn't be moved to endorse the advertising of any more than they would welcome getting relocated to Siberia.

Takeaways include:

- Generate likeability and preference through familiarity. Advertising's best approach is to use an existing zone of comfort to ease our natural fear of change.
- Neurologically, familiarity works because what's familiar is more accessible and doesn't require as much mental effort. In other words, it's easy.
- Familiarity also works because of lack of filtering. We're more accepting and emotionally invested in what's familiar to us. As a result, the brain unconsciously assumes that familiar information is true.
- To trigger the familiar-is-true-and-hence-acceptable formula, use repetition, casting choices that echo the target market and music that invokes appropriate associations.
- Beware of creating cognitive dissonance, because what goes against our preferred way of seeing things will create discomfort and, subsequently, be blocked from consideration as a way of protecting our own beliefs.

4

Focus on faces

ORIENTATION

People respond to people with emotions that are highly contagious. So selecting the right faces (and personalities) for ads is crucial, and yet nobody to date has really got much of a handle on it.

Surely there are many reasons why. But one of the main reasons has to be that the people who choose the talent and review the footage after a day's shoot most likely don't know facial coding. Over and above the type of physical look an agency may want for a campaign, there's also the matter of focusing on what types of expression will be appropriately on-emotion on behalf of the campaign. After all, a person's inherent emotive nature, expressive range and authenticity can make or break an advertising execution, as I have seen time and again.

The stakes couldn't be higher. The people who appear in ads become a big part of a company's brand personality, helping it to capitalize – or miss out – on an opportunity for us to relate to, identify with and ultimately have preference for the branded offer being advertised. The operative emotion for the viewer is curiosity, because in looking into someone's face, we prefer to believe, not unmistakenly, that we can catch a hint of what their personality is like as well.

WHY FACES ARE SPECIAL:
PROOF AND FOUR WELL-KNOWN REASONS

Imagine a company ranked well within the 100 largest in the United States, with sales of over $40 billion worldwide, and yet the faces of a few unknowns gain far more attention than the brand. That's what happened when we tested for an electronics retailer, whose TV spot had all sorts of brand elements clearly visible in it. The company's name appeared on the uniforms of employees, on products behind the employee spokespeople, as well as at the end of the commercial where, finally, based on eye tracking, at second 28, test participants fixated on the brand name and logo long enough to mentally register it.

Earlier, one, two, three, then a fourth employee, then a couple, an employee, the couple again, a family, the couple yet again, another employee, another couple, and the final employee: in all, some 16 seconds of video. And all the while, the gaze activity of test participants was at least 90 per cent concentrated on the faces of the people on screen. Indeed, the only significant departure from that pattern was that the guys we tested looked over the mother's bust line in the brief family scene.

Initially, the commercial was, in effect, an unbranded TV spot: first, the 16 seconds of looking at faces, followed by looking at numbers and key words in the copy on screen. How could it be that a commercial jammed with brand signifiers might not communicate its sponsor to viewers who didn't look away or leave the room before seconds 28 to 30? Moreover, in a country that watches as much television as we do in the United States, how could scene after scene with TV sets as the backdrop – sometimes a whole wall of the latest, greatest models – not draw people's eyes?

As that retailer learned, welcome to the power of faces.

In truth, the results were not a surprise to me. Our database of tested TV spots indicates that, based on eye-tracking results, faces are on screen 70 per cent of the time during TV spots and that 76 per cent of all the gaze activity while they're on screen is focused on faces. And that's just an average. If it weren't for cases where the talent is whirling around on screen, making it hard for consumers to track their faces, the average would be much higher. In point of fact, the retailer's spot was part of the 30 per cent of all TV spots we've tested where 80 to 95 per cent of the gaze activity is focused on the faces.

Faces: Earth's most important, mysterious surface

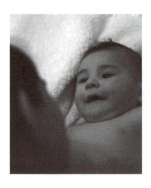

There is no single 'lying' muscle in the face. If there were, we would all probably be heading off to plastic surgeons or having Botox injections. But with facial coding, it is possible to pick up clues and insights into what others are feeling, a huge adaptive advantage honed over centuries. As the former US President Lyndon Baines Johnson reportedly once remarked, 'If you can't walk into a room and know who's with you and who's against you, you ain't worth spit as a politician.'

Why do we focus on faces, and do so right from birth? While this entire chapter is devoted to addressing that eternal mystery, let's start with some fairly obvious, well-known reasons why.

Faces are the sensory centre of our lives and the pre-eminent means of recognizing ourselves and others. For one thing, they're the place of four of our major sensory inputs: eyes, ears, nose and mouth. In addition, faces are an easy, immediate barometer by which we often gauge the health and vitality as well as beauty or handsomeness of another person.

Those reasons address the sensory aspect of faces. But there's also the emotional angle to consider in identifying and assessing others.

First, we focus on faces because they're so expressive, providing valuable information for anyone trying to read another person's mood and intent. Second, impressions drawn from people's facial expressions are often used to justify our opinions of new acquaintances. From 'shifty' looks, to 'kind' eyes or a 'crooked' smile, we don't hesitate to make character judgements based on what we see in somebody's face. In summary, as noted by social critic Roger Scruton, 'Human beings are alone among the animals in revealing their individuality in their faces.'[1]

WHY FACES ARE SPECIAL: SUBTLE FACTORS HIGHLY RELEVANT TO ADVERTISING

I've just provided obvious reasons why getting the use of faces right in advertising pays huge dividends. But there are other, subtle yet profound scientific factors at play here, too. I'll describe each factor in turn and state its implication for enhancing advertising's emotional strength.

For starters, face-reading and recognition are so vital to survival that there's a part of the brain especially devoted to reading other people's faces. It's called the fusiform face area (FFA), and is located near the visual-processing part of the brain, which is significant because an active face activates more of the brain.

Advertising implication: A changeable, emotive face provides motion, and people are geared to pay attention to motion. As the poet William Blake wrote: 'He who... acts not, breeds pestilence' (and I might add, unengaging advertising).

Second, the brain's FFA is a finely tuned instrument. Want to know how good it is? Look at the upside-down images of Mona Lisa on page 59. Then turn the page around. The distortions you almost certainly didn't notice before in her famous features went undetected because the brain reads an upside-down face as an object – leaving the visually acute FFA out of the process.

Order of visual processing of faces

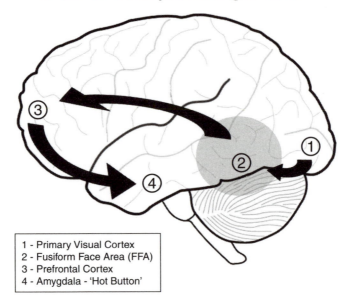

1 - Primary Visual Cortex
2 - Fusiform Face Area (FFA)
3 - Prefrontal Cortex
4 - Amygdala - 'Hot Button'

While the way we interpret faces does include step 3, where the brain's rationally oriented 'executive centre' provides input, the rest of the process is entirely sensory–emotive in nature. In other words, we respond to faces at a very intuitive gut level, judging whether somebody is a 'friend' or 'foe'.

Advertising implication: Compared with the power of faces, products, packages and other objects put in ads will tend to blunt engagement. So putting a single face, or two, but not nearly as many as the electronics retailer stuffed into its spot, in proximity to the key items in the ad will help to lift interest and cast a halo effect of visual attention onto them.

Third, a study of macaque monkeys may provide insights into human nature. Genetically almost identical to us, the macaques have 182 visual brain cells that are selectively responsive to faces or heads, but not to objects. Of these, 63 per cent are sensitive to head orientation and of those, nearly half are full-face oriented. As a result of studies with the monkeys, it's believed that to the degree that a face turns away from the viewer, human brain activity also most likely slackens.[2]

Advertising implication: From everything I've said, letting us see the actor's face seems obvious. But in testing a TV spot for Popeye's, for instance, Sensory Logic found that what was otherwise a successful commercial ended on an emotional low note because the actor was scripted to twirl, thus turning his back to the camera.

In an upside-down world, you're half-blind

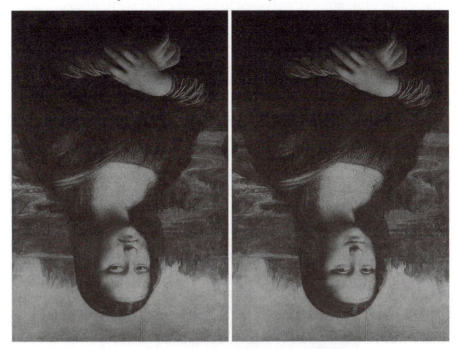

Before you flip the page around, Mona Lisa looks normal. You can't see the distortions. The reason is that object processing happens elsewhere in the brain, not in the facial-processing area. You're not able to scrutinize her face nearly as well when she's upside down because you're seeing her as merely an object.

Fourth, our face-reading ability is primarily a function of the right (emotional) hemisphere. The emotional significance of faces is revealed, in part, by research indicating that we can remember up to 10,000 faces.[3] Forget abstractions; seeing people moves us to feel. We also respond more to emotive faces than to neutral, expressionless faces. Furthermore, our right brain being more emotionally oriented means that, given the body's cross lateralization, the left side of our face is generally more expressive than the right side, especially when negative emotions are involved.

Advertising implication: If you're checking whether the smile on the person in the photo shoot isn't blemished by some negative feelings, check out the left side of their face first (unless they happen to be left-handed, in which case you most likely need to switch sides).

Fifth, facial expressions are emotionally contagious. Thanks to mirror neurons that read emotions and foster empathy, whatever somebody else feels and shows on their face, you also feel. Moreover, we tend to subconsciously adopt the expressions we detect in others because a perceived emotion activates the same brain circuits used to generate that identical emotion.

> *I like to see faces full of emotion. It becomes photographic when you see faces in motion. It would be morbid with a still face with no emotion. A face brings you in with excitement and something to share.*
>
> Katrin Nogols, Estonia

Advertising implication: Women tend to have not only more active mirror neuron responses, but also make more of the purchase decisions.[4] So isn't it downright foolish not to help make emotional responses contagious in your marketing efforts? This realization came to me a few years ago, during a project in which I found that a split-second look of fear on an actor's face (totally off-emotion and against the script, by the way) immediately took test participants there: they then felt fear, too.

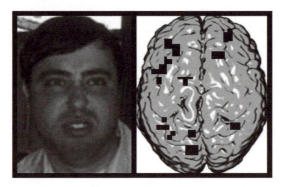

The man is showing some anger around the eyes. But much more pronounced is the disgust signalled by the raised, flaring upper lip. The image on the right shows the fMRI brain scan of a person whose feelings are being triggered by exposure to the photo on the left. What a match! That's because the second person's brain is lighting up in precisely the areas where disgust registers most strongly – evidence that emotions are as contagious as the flu.

Sixth and finally, familiar faces get stored in our brain's neural circuits in what's known as face-recognition units (FRUs). Every new face gets an intuitive FRU scan, as we look to make a match. Like memories, FRUs remain robust thanks to steady use, getting etched deeper into the brain through repetition. So-called 'warm' FRUs are why, for instance, a stranger with only a passing resemblance to the person you're madly in love with can trigger such a strong emotional response.

Advertising implication: Celebrity spokespeople can help because our emotionally oriented memory (the hippocampus) flares on seeing famous faces. On the other hand, is paying the big money for them necessary? Not exactly, for research indicates that the highly emotive faces of anonymous actors can spur more activity from our emotional hot buttons (our amygdalas). By the way, drawings of faces don't test well. So don't try saving on casting costs in that way.

> *If celebrities I like are in ads, it helps me to pay attention and I may have a better impression about the product or service. If celebrities I dislike are in ads, it also grabs my attention but then I tend to have a negative impression.*
>
> Rika Takahashi, Japan

FROM THEORY TO PRACTICE: EMOTIONAL RESPONSES TO FACES

Naturally, years of research using facial coding give us a unique vantage point from which to draw conclusions about what works and doesn't work, when it comes to how faces get used in advertising. Here's a little of what we've found:

1. Close-ups. In *Sunset Boulevard*, Gloria Swanson famously says: 'I'm ready for my close-up.' Are Hollywood and the directors of TV spots correct in using the close-up to move the audience? Based on moments in TV spots when there's a close-up versus its extreme opposite, a distant crowd shot, which grabs people the most (impact) and wins them over, creating preference (appeal)? The answer is the close-up, with a 20 per cent lift in appeal over and above the crowd shot's level of appeal. Moreover, the level of true-smile response (happiness) is nearly 10 per cent higher for close-ups over distant crowd shots.
2. Talent moving. Is a person merely talking on screen sufficiently involving, especially in comparison with a person actively moving around? The impact scores are identical, but appeal favours the actor being active when on camera in a TV spot.
3. Talent looking away. When it comes to reactions to head and face orientation, looking directly at the camera, face on, creates a response very similar to a 90-degree angle profile shot of the actor. But our seeing the

back of the actor's head results in both a notably lower impact score and a negative appeal score.

4. Gender. How about men versus women on screen? The response to a female presence is about even in terms of impact, but the appeal score is nearly 9 per cent higher than when men are on screen. (On a slightly different note, our database also reveals that when a lot of bare skin is showing, the appeal score reaches its highest level, a score of 26, with 43 per cent true-smile activity. So in other words, yes, sex sells.)

5. Famous faces. Finally, using famous people versus relatively unknown actors as talent merits hardly a difference emotionally, based on the results in our database. Famous faces achieve only slightly higher impact and appeal scores than their ordinary counterparts, who often try harder and are more emotionally engaged.

TRUE SMILES VERSUS SOCIAL SMILES: HOW HEARTFELT SMILES DIFFER FROM WILLED ONES

Over the centuries there have been all sorts of great quotes about faces. For instance, there's the observation by the Roman writer, Cicero: 'Everything is in the face.' Or this from the British writer, George Orwell: 'By the age of fifty a man has the face he deserves.' My favourite, though, is a rhetorical question from advertising legend Bill Bernbach: 'How do you storyboard a smile?'

Of course, in a way you don't; like any expression, a smile can't be described in words. Then again, thanks to the scientific rigour of facial coding it's possible to diagnose the differences between a number of smiles. Facial-coding guru Paul Ekman has described approximately 20 different types of smiles,[5] a few of which I'll review later on in the chapter.

That said, now let's focus on the gap between true smiles versus social smiles.

True smiles are innate and arrive first, soon after birth. (Later, between the fifth week and fourth month of life, the social smile appears.) Like the other core emotions, the happiness shown by a true smile isn't learned; it's automatic, beyond conscious control. Few of us can do even a halfway decent job of pretending to be genuinely, deeply happy when we're not. In contrast, with social smiles people are often faking.

As you may imagine, true smiles are better liked – hence the importance of learning this distinction for the purpose of making advertising that's on-emotion and connects well. In other words, make sure you use true smiles in your ads! By way of proof, social scientist Alicia Grandey and her colleagues ran a pair of tests.

Detecting a true versus a social smile

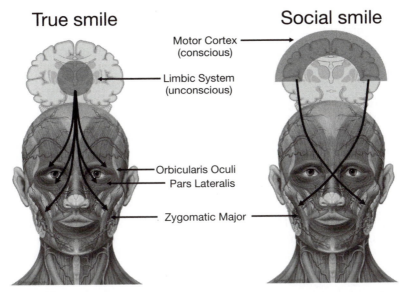

True smile   **Social smile**

True smiles emerge spontaneously from our intuitive limbic system and activate both the mouth and eye regions. The corners of the mouth rise, the cheeks rise, and there's a host of subtle muscle activity around the orbit of the eye socket. In contrast, Have-a-nice-day smiles involve a pathway from the motor cortex, appear only around the mouth and can be consciously summoned at will. The lack of eye-muscle activity is why we say, 'The eyes are the window to the soul,' a place where faking it doesn't come easily.

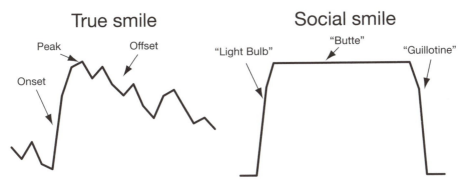

True smile   **Social smile**

Here's a further peek into my world of facially coding the rich and would-be powerful. When I critiqued the 2008 primary and presidential debates for CNN, Fox, MSNBC, NBC, Politico, and other media outlets, I had a field day with the politicians' often faked or contrived expressions of happiness.

In the first test, participants watched previously videotaped interactions that, unknown to them, had been staged between a hotel check-in clerk and a would-be guest. The variable was that for some check-in enactments the actress playing the clerk was invited to feel, then project, genuinely positive feelings toward the guest (true smiles). In other cases, the actress was instead told she had to smile (social smiles). Observers of the respective videos found the service performed with a truer smile far more satisfying.

The second test involved surveying random restaurant patrons after their meals. Those who felt the food servers' displays of positive feelings (ie smiles) were genuine reported far greater satisfaction with the service they had received.[6]

Given those stakes, it's understandable why General Mills has replaced the mythic happy housewife, Betty Crocker, with merely a spoon on its packaging. (There have been seven versions of Betty over the years, and in no version was she ever truly smiling.) That's because faked smiles can lead to frowns. In advertising, smiling people are a given. But the question is whether, in trying to leverage the cliché 'Smile, and the world smiles with you,' advertising falls afoul of the 21st-century emphasis on authenticity.

THE QUEST FOR AUTHENTICITY

Because authenticity is 'in' and fake is 'out,' a personality type that invites trust has become an asset. At the same time, however, the social smiles shown by CEOs, celebrities and others in today's advertising have become a serious liability. Fake feelings – especially of happiness, of unsubstantiated promises of hope – threaten faith in all advertising. A faked smile isn't on-emotion, thus off-target. Nobody wants to be spun or manipulated.

> *Our competitors for the most part I like to describe as a faceless family of people and what they are constantly trying to communicate is this sense of the power of the network. But it doesn't have a lot of personality in the way that our best work taps into an emotional level.*
>
> Denny Post, CMO, T-Mobile

Put another way, the stakes have increased. Twenty-first-century consumers often feel both wary and increasingly repulsed by what they perceive as corporate guile. Given the cynicism among today's media-savvy consumers, advertisers shouldn't risk showcasing the inauthentic feelings of paid actors. That's because everyone's naturally a facial coder. We all read other faces all the time, instinctively, inevitably, as people have done for centuries to aid in deciphering friends from foes.

How does the average consumer instinctively distinguish between true smiles and other, less than genuine, displays of pleasure? How can creative directors looking at photo-shoot output and video footage on the set be on guard against triggering negative emotional reactions in us because of false signals? Here's a primer:

- Social smiles tend to last an unnaturally long time. While a true smile will typically last for about four seconds – or even less – fake smiles don't know when to end. They linger. They're more like the Energizer bunny; they go on and on.
- Social smiles begin and end too abruptly or aren't in synch with what a person is saying. In short, they have odd timing.
- Social smiles are often asymmetrical, or lopsided, because they're being willed onto the face. As a result, whichever cerebral hemisphere is dominant will send a stronger signal. The left lip corner on a right-hander's face will rise higher, and the reverse for a lefty like me. In contrast, true smiles are involuntary expressions that occur in the older, emotional brain and exhibit a much more uniform onset, rise and peak of intensity, before they then fade.[7]

Of course, there are also other ways in which the viewers of everything from TV spots to print ads, direct-mail pieces, websites and outdoor can detect a note of emotional falsity. Since depictions of the happiness supposedly wrought by buying the product or service will be subject to intense scrutiny, bear in mind that false masking smiles are less likely to involve the full face. They may also come mixed with signs of other, darker, more negative emotions.

To that end, there are crocodile smiles (a mixture of happiness and contempt). In Japan, they're known as *nita-nita* or *chohshoh*. There are also grin-and-bear-it misery smiles (where the sun is out but it's also raining sadness), which I prefer to call Charlie Chaplin smiles because the famous silent-screen star's smile involved lips angling upwards more vertically than they do in a genuine smile. Finally, there's a range of smiles that cover up grim emotions. Who hasn't seen fearful, cringing smiles or cruel, angry smiles, among others?

CRITERIA FOR CASTING APPROPRIATELY AND EVALUATING PERFORMANCE

Finally, no discussion of focus on faces is complete without understanding the dynamics at work in choosing among four possible types of talent: celebrities,

CEOs (or other company leaders), professional experts and people giving testimonials or otherwise representing your typical consumer, ie Jane or Joe Doe. I am going to give you three criteria for evaluating the effectiveness of the people you choose to have on screen or in a photo shoot.

Communication experts will tell you that first and foremost is credibility.[8] Credibility comes from either *expertise* or common *experience*.

For a CEO or professional expert, such as a doctor giving a testimonial on behalf of a new medicine, expertise is crucial. They should know their stuff – from a rational, information-based perspective. In contrast, celebrities and Jane/Joe Doe consumers are effective based on the target market's gut-level emotional sense that what they are talking about is authentic and truly based on experience. For Jane or Joe Doe, our perception that they are informed through experience is a must-have; for celebrities, it's a nice-to-have quality that isn't quite as vital. Their star power can see them through here.

> *Sometimes the appearance of a celebrity may hurt the brand, because it is unbelievable that such a celebrity would use such a product. On the other hand, there is a particular brand of cookie in India sold at like $0.05 and I am convinced they are the best since the face of the cutest baby is on the advertisement!*
>
> Umang Talati, India

The second criterion is safety, which involves being trustworthy and likeable. Unlike the first criterion, safety is entirely emotional in nature. Here an ability to inspire trust is vital for CEOs and experts, whereas celebrities and the average Jane/Joe Doe consumer must score big on likeability.

The final criterion is dynamism, a quality that involves energy level or perceived power and prestige that, together, equate to status. Here, a high energy level is a desirable quality for celebrities and Jane or Joe Doe consumers, while status is mandatory for celebrities, CEOs and experts.

That's in theory. In practice, how well do actual CEOs and celebrities – the two most intriguing types of talent – do in adding emotional voltage to the ads they appear in? To find out, I decided to review examples of each.

> *Everybody is going to give you a smile. But celebrities don't cut it with young people, Coke is finding. Being part of the seed roots of music, that's far more significant than latching on to a celebrity who's already got lots of associations.*
>
> Paul Springer, author/consultant

I analysed the talent's facial expressions using two key criteria. First, are they emotionally expressive, hence engaging? Second, do they emote in an authentic manner that feels right because it fits the script and comes across as genuine? Let's see what I found, with ratings based on a 1/low to 5/high scale for measuring engagement and authenticity.

CEO	Engaging	Authenticity	Comments
Lee Iococca	2	2	The former Chrysler Chairman's smiles are far less genuine than Snoop Dogg's smirks
Dave Brandon / Domino's 'Big Taste Bail Out'	2	2	Words say anger about major companies getting bail-outs, but face is largely neutral
Dave Brandon / Domino's 'Burns Subway Letter'	5	4	Anger, sardonic disgust, and smiles in rejecting Subway's complaints, here the CEO is engaged
Dan Hesse / Sprint	2	5	Subdued smiles and smirks are genuine, but energy level doesn't match customers' service angst
Margaret Kelly / Remax Realty	3	2	A fair amount of (subdued) smiles, but they are tight and wan
Arkadi Kuhmann / ING 'Join the Savers'	1	1	Attempts body language (shrugs, etc.) but barely emotes and doesn't come across well
Jim McCann / 1-800-Flowers	3	1	Off-emotion: shows disgust, but he is selling the sweetness of flowers and saying all the right things
Average	2.57	2.43	

Is there room to improve the process of vetting the selection and performance of those who appear in front of the camera? As these results show, absolutely. To do so, choose talent based on video samples, instead of stills, as a starting point so that you get a better sense of the person.

Then after the video sessions (for TV spots), play the spot back three different ways: 1) with the sound off, so that you can concentrate on what the faces (and the other visuals) are conveying and whether it's on-emotion; 2) the sound by itself (does it match the visuals?); and 3) the TV spot played backwards (in scene-by-scene chunks) to make sure that the creative director's mind isn't artificially filling in gaps in narration/logic that, in reality, exist and will leave other people who see the spot perplexed. (Meanwhile, if it is photos you're critiquing, check them closely for the presence of less satisfying social smiles, or hints of other negative emotions in case they don't fit the purpose.)

Celebrity	Engaging	Authenticity	Comments
Sally Field / Boniva	4	4	Best moment is when she shows pride at fighting osteoporosis and does so genuinely; real smiles
Dennis Haysbert / Allstate	2	5	Doesn't emote a lot, but there are small smiles and a resolute look, supporting credibility – doesn't overplay it
Celine Dion / Chrysler	5	1	Lots of fake smiles get flashed; the car's smile (actually shown in the grille work) is more real
Julia Louis Dreyfuss / Healthy Choice	4	5	Constant eating holds down just how much she can emote (a little), but the disgust expressions, and puzzlement at being criticized for feeding her face, so on-emotion
Cindy Crawford / Pepsi	1	2	Barely emotes, with the "wow" of drinking Pepsi more in the eyebrows than the hint of a smile
Michael Jordan & Larry Bird / McDonalds	4/3	4/4	Jordan is more expressive, a mix of smiles, smirks and determination; Bird is emotionally monochromatic, either smiling or determined but never both at once
Drew Barrymore / Cover Girl	1	1	Lots of emoting, but the smiles fade quickly or linger, and lack a peak, revealing staged feelings

Overall, the celebrities came out best here: ahead of the CEOs by 35 per cent. Based on the two yardsticks of engaging and authenticity, the CEOs were harmed by a lack of authenticity in particular.

These are general recommendations. But two specific areas of improvement apply especially to the CEOs because, unlike celebrities on contract, they must be careful in serving as the enduring, public faces of their companies.

The degree to which CEOs prove to be engaging is the initial problem. After all, the law of emotional reciprocity is involved here: talent with an emotive, active face will, in turn, activate more engagement from the ad's viewers.[9] Or to put it in negative terms, coldness instinctively chills us – and for good reason. Psychopathic criminals (like some of those I've critiqued for CNN and Fox) are notable for having fMRI brain-scan results that indicate a lack of emotional activity. That's because these psycho killers have little response to the distress of others and are immune to remorse.

As a result, here's some blunt advice: don't use emotionally flat talent (even if it *is* the CEO), because you'll inadvertently create a psycho-killer brand!

Cold-hearted criminals also have cold minds

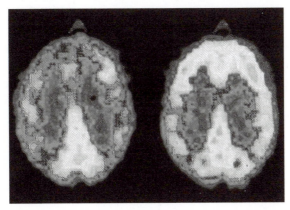

The fMRI brain scans shown here contrast the reaction of a typical, warm-hearted person (left brain) versus the lack of activity of a cold-hearted psychopath (right brain). In other words, if somebody 'gives you the chills', run, don't walk: your instincts are kicking in, helping to keep you alive.

SUMMARY

What's the takeaway here? Is it that studies that show that ads without faces attract less attention?[10] Is it that the people in ads who represent the brand well lift recall levels (the topic of my next chapter)?[11] Or is it the intriguing study that found that men pick up subtle signs of sadness in female faces only 40 per cent of the time whereas women do so at a 90 per cent accuracy rate?[12]

Really, it's all of those angles and more because in advertising the human face represents a treasure trove of opportunity to engage us and compel consideration and persuasion. To neglect or otherwise under-utilize the power of faces, such as by being off-emotion, is as much a handicap as a guy who can't see that his romantic date for the evening is feeling unhappy. Don't go there.

Takeaways include:

- Over and above the type of physical look, in casting focus on what types of expressions will be appropriately on-emotion on behalf of the campaign. After all, the talent's inherent emotive nature, expressive range and authenticity can make or break an advertising execution.
- Approximately 75 per cent of all gaze activity will be focused on faces when they're on screen. We focus on faces because they're the sensory centre of our lives, and a way to read another person's mood and intent.

- A changeable, emotive face provides motion, and people are geared to pay attention to motion. Moreover, facial expressions are emotionally contagious and a way to boost engagement. As a result, use close-ups and avoid back-of-the-head shots.
- True smiles are better received than forced smiles that involve less of the face because fake feelings leave us feeling manipulated.
- Talent credibility depends on dynamism or engagement being shown, as well as being on-emotion and authentic. CEOs need to be careful that they don't just convey expertise, and thus come across as emotionally flat.

5

Make it memorable

ORIENTATION

While the first job of advertising is to get itself noticed, the second job is to be remembered. That outcome is vital to commerce but isn't well served by existing recall methods that haven't got around the problem of what people can't or won't say. What's wrong with using verbal feedback, or ratings? The scientific reality is that recall isn't an intellectual process. Instead, generating memories that inspire recall is an emotional-driven process that by and large happens subconsciously.

Picture a network of neurons that get activated like a string of firecrackers that go *bang*, setting off neighbouring neurons. That's closer to reality and why the vital few seconds during the first exposure to an ad are most likely to determine if there's been a spark of delight, or at least interest.

DID YOU SEE IT?
RECALL MEASURES AS A HOUSE OF MIRRORS

We're now almost halfway through *About Face*. So it's time for a little quiz. Only it won't be about what you've learned – and retained – so far in reading this book. Instead, it's about how recall has been traditionally tested by market researchers judging the effectiveness of advertising. Here's my quiz for you.

Quiz (multiple choice)

1. Compare the likely impact of two anti-smoking, public-service TV spots.

    Descriptions: One spot ('Truth') shows teenagers piling body bags in front of a tobacco company's headquarters. Voices amplified by megaphones tell viewers that these body bags represent the 1,200 people killed daily by smoking. In effect, 'Truth' portrays teenagers as heroes, asserting their independence against a destructive product (tobacco). A comparative spot ('Think), ie 'Think. Don't smoke,' seeks to reduce tobacco usage by recycling the same old 'Just say no' message of yesteryear.

    Based on these descriptions, which TV spot would you expect to be more effective? (Choose one.)

    A. 'Truth'
    B. 'Think'

2. Identify which recall level makes sense for these two spots.

    Levels based on unaided awareness vs. aided recall: 'Truth' is remembered by either 21.9 per cent of its target market or 74.9 per cent – a 53 per cent difference. 'Think' is remembered by either 3.2 per cent or 65.5 per cent of its target market – a 62.3 per cent difference. Measured one way (unaided awareness), the two campaigns register an 18.7 per cent difference in recall rates. Measured another way (aided recall), the difference is merely 9.4 per cent. Can you reconcile these varying figures? *What in the world is going on here, anyway?*

    Based on the two spots described, which recall levels strike you as most likely?

    (Choose two, one selection for 'Truth' and one for 'Think'.)

    A. For 'Truth', 21.9 per cent unaided recall
    B. For 'Truth,' 74.9 per cent aided recall
    C. For 'Think,' 3.2 per cent unaided recall
    D. For 'Think,' 65.5 per cent aided recall

3. Identify which recall level makes sense, on average.

    Different average recall levels, based on results from different databases: The typical level of advertising recall is 25 per cent. In regard to TV spots, recall is 67 per cent, no, make that 7 per cent. Which of these numbers, if any, actually makes sense to you? How confident does this wide range make you feel?

    Given all the advertising people see, which recall level strikes you as reasonable?

    (Choose one.)

A. 25 per cent average recall
B. 67 per cent average recall
C. 7 per cent average recall

4. Recall testing as currently practised is excellent because (choose one option that sounds valid based on the descriptions below):

A. Unaided recall – whereby the tester mentions a brand and asks the test participant to provide any recent examples of advertising for the brand – won't be distorted by judgment calls. Don't worry that testers must decide whether the advertising execution, as described by the participant, fits well enough to qualify as 'recall' of it.
B. Aided recall – whereby the tester describes the ad to see if the test participant can confirm awareness of it – won't be affected by semantics or human nature. In regards to semantics, how ads get described by the tester remains consistent and neutral. In regards to human nature, don't worry that research suggests the average person lies three times per every ten minutes of conversation. Surely, the participant will signal 'yes' to having seen an ad only when that is truly the case.
C. Conscious confirmation suffices. The brain-science studies indicating that most mental processing of advertising occurs on a subconscious, emotional basis and, therefore, couldn't be easily confirmed through conscious, rationally oriented, verbal input are hogwash.
D. Vested interests aren't a problem. Just because the major market research firms have historical databases they want to insist are valid isn't a cause for concern. The classic story of the emperor's new clothes is an amusing tale but it doesn't apply to business because big companies never try to lock in the status quo.
E. None of the above.

Best answers: 1: A; 2: A and C; 3: C; 4: E.

EXPLAINING THE ANSWERS: THE GAP BETWEEN RECALL AND HOW AD RETENTION WORKS

What are the major takeaways from this quiz? First, in regards to recall testing, it's that aided recall levels strike me as preposterous. Given all the advertising that people get exposed to, how likely is it that on average the aided recall of 'Truth' (74.9 per cent) and 'Think' (65.5 per cent) is 70.2 per cent? No way.

After all, in regards to question 3, the average recall levels quoted there vary from 7 per cent to 67 per cent – a range of 60 per cent. With that range, it's hard to trust any of the results. But given the degree to which we're saturated with advertising, I suspect the lower end of the range is more accurate. Note that research data from Burke on US recall levels way back in 1990 had already dipped to 4 per cent,[1] an amount not far off from the 3.2 per cent unaided recall level recorded for Philip Morris's undistinguished 'Think' campaign.

Second, even if the unaided recall approach provides a better, more reliable means of gauging how memorable an ad is than aided recall, the results are still likely to be deeply flawed. That's because of how memory works. In essence, it's emotive in nature (unlike recall testing, which depends on language skills located in the rational part of our brains). Notable impressions are much more likely to turn into lasting memories if they relate to our previously stored experiences, based on a retention process that unfolds in three stages: encoding, storage and retrieval.

Encoding depends on the sensory bandwidth getting engaged. A visual impression enters our 'sensory store' for about half a second, and up to five seconds for auditory input. If it's not then chosen to be processed further, a given piece of sensory data disappears, written over by the new sensory input that's constantly arriving. Only a fraction of the sensory information we take in gets moved to active memory – typically because the information is relevant to our goals and needs, and/or because the information involves novelty, change and intensity.

For novelty and intensity, it's hard to beat death

Driving while drunk isn't necessarily much better than driving while dead tired, leading to being, well, just simply dead, period. This is one of numerous public-safety ads of this type that have run in New Zealand in recent years.

The storage of memories follows, in turn, based on the degree to which the information is associated with or linked to what else we've already retained. The greater the number and intensity of these links, the better the storage of information will be (which is why the rule covered in Chapter 3, 'Keep it close to home', is well worth adhering to).

> *I think that using the essence of the product or service as a basis for your ad is crucial, especially for recall. Ads that use 'borrowed interest' or in other words make up scenarios that don't spring from the product mean less to people and are easy to confuse with other products in the category. Beer advertising falls into this a lot; it's really not about the brand or product so much as who can come up with the funniest commercial.*
>
> **Scott Mackey, creative director, Mackey, Inc.**

For example, it's an urban legend that Santa Claus was invented by Coca-Cola or that Santa wears red and white clothing because those are Coke's colours. In reality, the red-suited Santa was a creation of the 19th-century US cartoonist Thomas Nast. But what *is* true is that through Coke's massive Christmas advertising during the 1930s, the company was able to popularize what are now our collective associations – and memory – of Santa as wearing red and white, whereas prior to Coke's campaigns he wore a variety of colours.

The advantage for Coca-Cola is that it played to attributes already there in people's minds because there's a rich, varied assortment of mental imagery related to Santa Claus spread out across the history of Western culture. In contrast, most taglines are throwaways because they lack both emotional hooks and common sense. (What did Mobil's entry of 'We want you to live' mean anyway?)

Finally, retrieval involves intuitively, subconsciously searching our own associative memory network for specific information relevant to the new input. A match between what's new and the old memory reactivates what's already stored – and becomes an argument in favour of using repetition in advertising, since memories form when a pattern is repeated frequently. Moreover, each time a group of neurons fires together the tendency to do so again is increased.[2] In essence, having a handle on a piece of information based on a previous context makes it easier to grab and use again, while also framing how it will be interpreted.

EXPLAINING THE ANSWERS:
WHY 'TRUTH' WON AND WHAT IT MEANS FOR YOU

Is there another big takeaway from this chapter's opening quiz (besides the suspect nature of traditional recall testing)? Yes, there is and it has to do with how you create memorable ads. In a word, it's all about leveraging emotion.

Among the numerous recall numbers you saw, one of them actually makes sense. It's the relative gap between how 'Truth' performed against 'Think' based on unaided recall. Forget the numbers themselves for each spot. It's the relative gap between them that I'm interested in. Yes, no doubt the non-profit, anti-smoking 'Truth' campaign should emerge as more memorable, more striking, by a ratio of about 10 to 1, because it's visual and emotional (the body bags) compared to the Philip Morris Company's rationally oriented 'Think' campaign.

> *Advertising boils down to a dramatic demonstration or a dramatic metaphor. Recall is all about the drama created.*
>
> **Larry Kelley, creative director, FKM Agency**

'Truth' speaks to emotionally laden values, and taps into the instinctive youthful attitude of rebelling against authority. In comparison, 'Think' is aptly named – and yet Philip Morris knows how to do better. It's just that in this case it presumably didn't want to do so. Indeed, since the researchers for this project were academics working for the altruistic American Legacy Foundation, we know from their findings that the target market of 12- to 17-year-olds exposed to 'Think' actually became *more* open to the idea of smoking (contrary to what happened to youths exposed to 'Truth').

Surely Philip Morris signed off on creative that enabled it to accomplish what it wanted, ie to suppress rather than inspire recall. A look at the phenomenal success of the Marlboro Man campaign is proof that Philip Morris knows how to achieve the opposite effect – a highly memorable campaign – by leveraging emotion when it wants to do so.

Back then, what was the nature of the company's advertising strategy? *Pure emotion.* Rugged. Tough. Independent. Make younger people, especially guys, respond by wanting to be brand-loyalty cowboys. Before the campaign created by the Leo Burnett agency started in 1959, Marlboro was a flagging brand marketed through the usual features and benefits: fine blend, good taste, etc. Then, with the new campaign from Burnett, Marlboro's parent company:

- stopped selling the cigarette's features and benefits and started selling *desire*... What do teenage boys want? Not cigarettes. They want respect, pride, a strong self-image, and girls. Unfortunately, cigarettes don't contain any of those features or benefits.

● Thus was born the rugged Marlboro Man… You didn't need to tell boys and young men about special blends. They didn't care, and had proved it by not buying Marlboro in the past. Now, when a boy bought Marlboro, he wasn't buying cigarettes; he was buying a feeling of manhood. The cigarette was just the means to that end.[3]

How successful was taking an emotional route? So successful that when Sensory Logic tested the emotional brand equity of some leading brands a few years ago, 100 per cent of the men we tested were emotionally engaged by the Marlboro brand – despite an advertising ban for tobacco in general that's now existed for decades. Can you really imagine that Philip Morris misunderstood or forgot this valuable lesson about leveraging emotions?

The answer is, no, as further proved by still more evidence of the effectiveness of 'Truth':[4]

● When the American Legacy Foundation's researchers asked teenagers if they were likely to smoke a cigarette during the upcoming year, 66 per cent of those exposed to 'Truth' said 'less likely' while 36 per cent of those exposed to 'Think' said 'more likely'.
● The 'Truth' campaign launched in Florida first. Two years later (probably helped by a rise in the state's cigarette taxes), smoking by high-school students had fallen by 18 per cent and by middle-school students by a whopping 40 per cent.
● It was the settlement of a multitude of anti-tobacco lawsuits that had made possible the funding for the 'Truth' campaign. But as part of the settlement, the tobacco industry was given some veto powers over how the settlement monies could be spent on an anti-smoking campaign. Why mention that fact? Because the industry soon objected to the 'Truth' campaign and forced it off the air, blunting its impact.

In the end, the tobacco industry described the 'Truth' ad as 'inconsistent' with the mission of the settlement-funded American Legacy Foundation. But was it? Or was the ad actually highly consistent with the goal of preventing smoking among teenagers, which it did by sparking rebellion: transforming an instinct to be the (Marlboro) Man into wanting to rebel against the Man, instead?

Sad song of the smoking cowboy

As anybody who knows Westerns well realizes, good guys wear white cowboy hats while the bad guys dress in black. But is it always that simple? After all, sometimes the good guys are 'square' and the bad guys are really good at heart. In this case, the protruding cigarette seeks to link the mythology of free-range cowboy with outlaw rebel. It's powerful stuff. But so is the anti-smoking 'Truth' ad that seems to have taken on mythology and won, making tobacco companies the equivalent of those who take the freedom of having your health away from you.

THREE ADDITIONAL CRITERIA FOR ENHANCING AD RETENTION BASED ON HOW MEMORY WORKS

To improve the odds that your advertising will be memorable, there are eight guidelines worth following. Under the general guideline of leveraging emotion, five have already been introduced:

- Relevancy. Establish a relationship to goals, involving fears, needs and wants. More about this will be said in Chapters 6 and 7.
- Novelty. What's new leverages natural curiosity.
- Change. Real or implied motion gets our attention because change may provide opportunities or pose a threat.
- Intensity. What's 'red-hot' invites or even demands scrutiny.
- Familiarity. Memory is aided by leveraging associations, ie what's already well known through frequency and recency. Link a key fact to some meaningful memory and use the latter to hook us on the former.

That leaves three more guidelines that I want to explore here, especially in regards to TV and radio spots. They are: pacing, peaks and patience.

Pace (how too much leads to too little emotional response)

Let's start with pace, which is in large part about the need for simplicity. The reality is that many ads put too much of a mental strain on us. As Robert Heath has noted in a recent edition of *Admap*, a major problem with traditional recall measures is that in being rationally oriented they fail to take into account that most of our processing of ads actually happens in a peripheral, subconscious mental processing style.[5] To do it otherwise quickly overloads us, as 95 per cent of people's thought activity actually happens on an intuitive, subconscious level.

In other words, make us consciously work too hard and we burn out, undermining the opportunity for recall. Here's a case in point. We've gone through our project files to identify the number of emotional data points (moments of emotional engagement) that occur in various TV or radio spots in relation to the number of scenes in a given spot. By scenes, I mean cuts and edits involving a fairly significant change in factors such as the content, scene, camera angle or use of voices, among other possibilities. The table on page 80 shows what we've found.

As you can see from the data, you do best when you have three or four scenes in a spot. Fewer scenes and the spot is too static and dull. More than that and the emotional response level drops off as we scramble to keep abreast of what's happening. In keeping with Wundt's Curve (see Chapter 4), our

It's not just you: yes, the pace is too quick

Number of Scenes	Data Point %
1-2	33%
3-4	*40%*
5-6	33%
7+	26%

What the chart shows is the percentage of seconds during a TV or radio spot that get an emotional data point. The sweet spot is to have three or four scene changes. Go beyond that level and the patient (the target market) begins to slide toward a cardiac arrest.

results show that to achieve the most engagement, a little complexity is good; a lot of complexity is commercial poison and erases the sweet spot of offering either simplicity and novelty or a little complexity along with what's familiar.

Two additional, related insights consist of the following:[6]

- For greater recall, place key information after a scene change that is related, in content, with the scene before. That way, you gain the advantage of novelty (the scene change) but keep it simple by maintaining the content's focus. On the other hand, don't put key information after unrelated, content-shifting cuts that increase the mental effort required of us. While the right degree of novelty and change orients our attention, too much of it will overload us.
- Fast-paced TV spots tend to draw involuntary attention (and recall) to sensory elements such as the actors, action, scenery and music. So fast-paced spots work great for brand and imagery advertising, but not so well for spots where the intent is to create recall of persuasive messaging delivered through words spoken or shown on screen.

Peaks (without high points, everything's flat)

Second, research indicates that success – as well as high recall – comes from leveraging the reality that people remember openings, peaks and endings in advertising, as in life in general. Here I want to address the timing of peak emotional responses during funny ads, because both surprise and humour/happiness peaks are involved.

A few years ago, a trio of academics decided to find out if their hypotheses about how humour works in advertising were correct.[7] In their case, test participants used a computer mouse to track their reactions to 15 humorous versus 15 other TV spots. In contrast, my staff reviewed a combination of 25 TV and radio spots we consider funny. Then we used our facial-coding results to understand how test subjects reacted on a more intuitive, emotional level.

In theory, it's best if the surprise peak comes late in the TV spot but ahead of the humour peak. Their study reported that a surprise/humour-peak scenario happened in that order 86 per cent of the time. Our study found that to be rarely true (36 per cent). In other words, two-thirds of the time the peak of humour and happiness came before the surprise-reaction peak.

In theory, it's also best if the surprise peak comes late in the TV spot. While the other study found no difference in people's enjoyment of TV spots with early or late surprise peaks, our study found that intense happiness was 13 per cent more common when the surprise peak came during the back half of the TV spot. In other words, delay the peak of surprise and the happiness you're more likely to recall later will be more intense.

Now let me explain the implications for achieving greater recall levels.

Our results showed that, yes, the more the peaks come close together the better the emotional chain reaction. Moreover, we've found a potentially interesting statistical coincidence. Remember the Burke data I cited earlier in this chapter, suggesting recall levels under 5 per cent? Well, in Sensory Logic's case, our review of peak points has found that 80 per cent of the TV and radio spots we've tested have a single peak moment of emotional response. Meanwhile, another 15 per cent of these spots enjoy two peaks, *with the remaining 5 per cent achieving three or more peaks.* Could it be that funny ads – and all ads – require three peaks or more to achieve recall? I think that might well be true.

> *The most distinct ad I've seen is for the VW Touareg, of a rebellious kid whom his father has decided to take on a country drive and just share the experience of being together. I love it because it's a beautiful story (ends with the boy throwing his arm around the dad as they take a picture next to the car), and secondly it's real. This is what parents experience, and I would try it if I had a son like him.*
>
> Themba Ndlovu, South Africa

Moreover, the question then arises: are they good peaks? Yes: 88 per cent of all these peaks were predominantly positive – with happiness outweighing negative emotions, and frustration levels far below what we normally see in TV and radio spots overall. So peak experiences seem to tilt positive, which is great for achieving both recall *and* emotional buy-in from consumers. As to what tactically contributes to, or causes, these peaks, here's what we found (ranked based on ability to generate a positive emotional outcome):

Causation	Appeal	Impact	True Smiles	Frustration	% Positive Emotion
Motion/Action	33.6	36.9	51.0%	5.2%	87.8%
Animation/Special Effects	31.0	35.9	45.6%	9.8%	83.7%
Singing/Sound Effects	27.3	33.7	38.2%	13.2%	77.7%
Punch Line	23.8	32.5	37.2%	15.7%	71.9%
Enthusiasm/Excitement	22.3	29.6	30.4%	16.4%	72.8%

To summarize, people dancing and jumping around (*motion/action*) really works, no matter how hare-brained. Words moving in *animated* fashion across the screen or other special visual effects are the second most reliable contributor to positive peak responses. Pretty close behind are *singing and sound effects* used, especially in radio. *Punchlines* – the focus of many a copywriter's long days – are a distant fourth. Finally, talent *exhibiting passion* through louder voices and emoting faces is fifth.

Study that list, and you'll be a wiser, richer marketer. No formula, in and of itself, is the answer. But going with peak moments to achieve recall and sales success is a good place to start.

Patience (a spot's plot needs time to build properly)

Especially in a business cycle in which the economy is weak, it becomes tempting to opt for creating – and paying – for shorter spots to run on TV and radio. But in terms of robust results, leading to greater recall potential, is it a case of cutting off your nose to spite your face, saving money only to waste the money you're still spending? Based on our results for the two media, we believe the answer is yes.

When translated into percentages, on average a 15-second TV spot generates only 64 per cent as much appeal as a 30-second spot and only 89 per cent as much impact. Meanwhile, on average a 30-second radio spot generates only 84 per cent as much appeal as a 60-second spot while near the mark with 98 per cent as much impact. In conclusion: quite often, haste makes waste.

Further proof that a TV or radio spot needs time to build its story comes from another way that we've reviewed our results. In this case, we focused on where the largest volume of emotional response typically occurs during a spot. The answer? It doesn't come early, so be patient. In fact, it occurs during seconds 21 to 25 most of all, when the spot's plot resolution is typically occurring. Close behind is the span from seconds 11 to 15, when the plot often undergoes a twist. In contrast, the opening five seconds are akin to being in the threshold of a store: a place where few (emotional) sales get made, but that we must pass through in order to buy.

So far, so good: these data largely fit what advertisers might expect and want – with one major exception. And that's how the volume of emotional response falls slightly toward the end of a spot, when the attempt is made to 'close the deal'. Since it's during the closing that the brand is typically on screen in TV spots or being spoken of during radio spots, let's now end the chapter by turning to brand recall.

It's a crucial issue given that a major review of in-market sales effects, across nearly 400 test markets, 'found no evidence of a relationship between related recall scores and sales effects for either new products or established brands'. Indeed, in recognizing the need for emotion to be front and centre as part of the recall picture, that same article by Charles Young, founder and CEO of Ameritest, then concludes: 'It appears that the widely used report-card measure of day-after recall does not capture the potential sales impact of emotion in advertising.'[8]

HOW TO AVOID THE RISK OF CREATING UNBRANDED ADS

Expanding on Young's point, Rex Briggs and Greg Stuart pointedly refer to research showing that 'the predicator of sales success is *not ad awareness recall*; it is the *meaning* consumers attach to the brand'.[9] But even more basic is a problem confronting, not researchers tracking recall levels, but ad agencies and their clients. It's brand recall levels, period. Put simply: they're appalling. Companies are running ads and nobody remembers the sponsor. Clearly, brand linkage must be improved.

> *Usually, I don't notice the brand names in advertising unless I already knew them. However, when I already knew the brand name, it is because I have seen them outside like in the train or billboard aside of the road. When I can remember them, it has a memorable symbol of company or a noticeable tagline of its products.*
>
> Sadoaki Takata, Japan

How much so? In *Emotionomics*,[10] I cited research that correct brand recall happens only in about 25 per cent of all advertising. According to the source on which I drew,[11] nearly half of all ads aren't recognized, another 18 per cent are recognized but the brand (sponsor) isn't recalled, and 12 per cent of the time the wrong brand is recalled. Needless to say, those aren't encouraging numbers. To prompt us to consider the category of goods but not a specific offer isn't worthwhile. Nor is remembering only the ad's other, non-branded, content, because the goal here isn't to spur us to buy the ads themselves.

As I noted in Chapter 2, when it comes to forms of advertising like print ads, for instance, the problem in large part lies in putting the logo in the lower right corner, ie the corner of death. It's the second-to-last place most of us look in scanning a print ad.

How about in TV spots, however? In their case, the logo gets placed typically right in the middle of the screen. So relocating the logo isn't a solution. What might be? To help figure out ways to enhance brand linkage, Sensory Logic checked its project files to identify the volume of emotional engagement – feeling points – that are happening while at least one of three conditions is being met:

- A company's logo is on screen, and the focal point.
- There's a product shot with the company logo clearly visible, and the product shot is the focal point (to guard against viewers being distracted by, say, people on screen).
- The company name and, optionally, its tagline, too, are the focal point.

> *I remember ads that you cannot guess the brand until they show them. But I must confess that I cannot remember most of the brands of my favorite ads.*
>
> Nina Arends, Uruguay

Based on the emotional engagement while the logo is on screen, typically three to seven seconds at the end of a TV spot, shown below the chart's clear image of the Golden Gate Bridge are the top four ways in which engagement gets a lift. The approaches are listed in descending order based on the volume of engagement they generate.

The first item aside, the best way to boost engagement is for the logo to be linked to action. In comparison, below the foggy image of the Golden Gate Bridge are the weaker ways of handling a logo. They involve only half to one-fifth as much engagement as the top four options, and again are listed in descending order based on the volume of engagement they generate.

What do these seven approaches have in common, and why are they so much weaker than the first four options? As to commonality, two qualities stand out most. One is greater complexity. The second is that the logo appears in static form, rather than in motion, whether in the foreground, background or by itself.

Are additional approaches valuable, or perhaps even required, to ensure that brand linkage will improve? Yes, that's true. Who knows what all the tactical tricks and tips might be? But one thing is certain: great brand recall will be aided by great brand equity because we remember what matters to us, a reality that Apple, for instance, takes to the bank every day.

- Logo appears alone right after the punch line gets delivered
- Logo gets animated, either emerging, fading or filling in from left to right
- Action on screen interactively involves the logo in some way
- Ongoing action, with logo superimposed over the action

- Screen contains logo, other text, and people
- Logo embedded into action, appearing as part of the background 'scenery'
- Combination of text, company's website and logo
- Quick, static logo shot
- Introduction of music accompanies logo's appearance on screen
- Final scene freezes, serves as a background on which logo gets superimposed
- Logo appears/lingers middle of screen as static image

SUMMARY

Memory is at once both selective and reconstructive. We tend to remember the gist of something, but the details fade or change. Information that gets emotionally tagged will at least stand a better chance than trying to overload us with a white-noise blur of rational messaging alone. Advertisers shouldn't forget that we encode, store and retrieve what fits most comfortably into an existing mental framework. We remember what we internalize, and what we internalize is part of us, and what is part of us is an opportunity a company can sell us on again and again.

Therefore, brand equity becomes decisive just when recall is of greatest value to a company. That's the moment of choice, whether enacted with a mouse click online or in a store or showroom. Then the sum of past experiences and associations determines our feelings for the brand, an emotional verdict on which is likely to hang the purchase decision.

Takeaways include:

- While recall has traditionally been tested by rational means, the scientific reality is that recall isn't an intellectual process. Instead, it's emotional in nature and mostly happens on a subconscious basis.
- Only a fraction of the sensory information we take in gets moved to active memory, typically because the information has one or more of the

following qualities: relevancy, novelty, intensity, familiarity, and/or involves change.

- Another key factor, related to simplicity, is pacing. The optimal number of scenes in a TV or radio spot is three or four in order to achieve the maximum amount of emotional response, which in turn facilitates recall potential.

- The other two recall factors are peaks and patience. Sensory Logic results suggest that increasing the number of emotional peaks is probably tied to recall, with three peaks being optimal. Patience is advised in that shorter executions may cost less to air but rob the creative of time to build creative punch.

- Brand recall levels are appallingly low. Ways to boost those levels include: having the logo appear right after the punchline, animated logos, interactive logos, or ongoing action with the logo superimposed over the action.

6

Relevancy drives connection

ORIENTATION

In pursuit of sales, it's almost inevitable that the company seeking to advertise its products or services – its offers – wants to emphasize features and attributes, believing the offer to be the hero. Or the price if the company sees itself as trapped in the commodity zone because the offer isn't unique and distinguished enough to be the hero.

But the place to start is to step closer to the target market. To do that requires acknowledging the problem/solution storyline that must underline any offer. In Chapter 7, my emphasis will be on the solution. But here in this chapter, the focus is on the problem: what makes us sad and what makes us hope for happiness. A goal of advertising must, therefore, be to make the problem vivid enough that we will be drawn in and ready to accept the offer's value. In short, with advertising's help the offer is still the hero. But it's the hero based on what it will do to solve problems and address people's *emotional* needs, rather than the functional, utilitarian view of the offer that the company is naturally most focused on.

THE CATEGORICAL TRUTH: NEVER FORGET THE WIIFM

One of the funniest and most incisive passages in Al Ries and Jack Trout's book, *Positioning*, is when they attack the conventional logic that says 'You find your concept inside yourself or inside the product.' 'Not true,' they reply. 'What you must do is look inside the prospect's mind. You won't find an "uncola" idea inside a 7Up can. You find it inside the cola drinker's head.'[1]

The bottom line here is that in advertising it always comes back to the WIIFM: the consumer asking themselves, 'What's in it for me?' A company can't sell a solution nearly as easily, consistently, or for as much money unless it first establishes the substance of the problem to be solved. Yes, there are both needs and wants – a distinction I will return to shortly. But first there is the underlying problem (or unfulfilled desire) that is responsible for the product or service category even existing.

What's the best way to ensure relevancy? It's to review the problem/solution format that underlies the product/service category. Why did the category come into existence? What need or want or fear does it address? And has the category's emotional reason for being changed over the years? As copywriter Luke Sullivan notes, in starting with a clean sheet of paper it's always a good idea to 'Find the central human truth about your whole product category. The central *human* truth.'[2]

Look for the essence of what the category is about. Hair colouring isn't really about looking younger; it enhances *self-esteem*. Getting a Harley-Davidson motorcycle isn't really about affordable transportation; it expresses *freedom*. Daughters may beg for a cellphone, explaining it's for security; but it's really so they can *bond* with their friends.

Marketing 101: follow their self-interest, not yours

What are the new social media about? It's often 'we', but it's even more often about 'me'. It's *my* blog, *my* posted photos of *my* vacation, etc. Naturally, a satirical backlash has set in.

Addressing the WIIFM is always smart. A case in point: one of my favourite *New Yorker* cartoons shows two women talking, with one saying to her companion: 'But enough about me. What do you think about me?' While nobody at birth needs or wants a particular product or service, our own private needs, wants and fears resonate deep inside us.

It's no surprise that in the study cited earlier in this book, Yale University concluded that atop its list of the 12 most persuasive words in the English language is 'you', as in 'You'll be glad you bought this' or other copy that addresses the target market in personal terms.[3]

So, how do companies go about advertising? Do they use 'you', and how often? Do they get beyond their own WIIFM to talk to ours? To find out, my staff looked over 75 ads, equally split between print, TV and radio. In 25 print ads, there were 20 uses of 'you' in total: an average of less than one use per print ad for the single most persuasive word in the English language! How about TV? With 23 total uses, the results were only nominally better. Fortunately, here's where radio shone, relatively speaking, with 77 uses – better than three 'yous' per radio spot.

Not definitive data? True, but they're in line with the equally informal survey done by the authors of *The Little Blue Book of Advertising*. In Lance and Woll's case, they concluded that some 80 to 90 per cent of all ads tilt away from being user-benefit oriented, away from you and your WIIFM, and unfortunately toward mere corporate chest-pounding ('Aren't we terrific?') instead.[4]

TYPES OF MOTIVATIONS:
A SERIOUS CASE OF WANTING FUN FOOD

The words *motivation* and *emotion* come from the same Latin word, *movere*, which means 'to move'. As my next diagram shows, the ideal spot a company's advertising should occupy is the top right quadrant, leveraging motivations in order to be persuasive, rather than merely providing educational, on-message information.

Our emotions turn on when a need, want or fear is at stake. Remember that because only the sensory–emotive parts of the brain attach to muscle activity, emotional response and a strong connection are vital to driving both consideration and persuasion. Sales happen due to the influence of emotions. To that end, creativity in an advertising context should be redefined as the *creation* of emotions in us that promote consideration rather than rejection of an advertised offer.

> *If an advertisement hits to the sentiments of family or what family is defined by, I will be easily persuaded. For example, I am still very loyal to a certain brand of flour because the advertisements I remember growing up were of an entire family sitting down to dinner and having a wonderful meal, and they were all happy and the tagline said something like…happy families all use this brand of flour.*
>
> Umang Talati, India

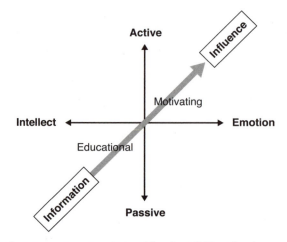

Where does being on-message sit in this chart? Try the lower left quadrant: information. Where does being on-emotion fit? Yes: the much more desirable upper right quadrant, where you use your advertising to influence the outcome you want (sales). Along the way, you climb from what's educational to what's motivating – the vital topic of this chapter.[5]

Take the case of an award-winning radio spot on behalf of Pirro Brothers Pizza. In it a young boy wants pizza. He wants pizza. He wants pizza *soo* bad...well, let's listen in as the announcer puts the boy's plight in the context of how to write a good radio spot:

Announcer: Advertising is simple. First, you must grab their attention.
Boy: Mom!
Announcer: Give them strong, supporting copy.
Boy: I'm hungry.
Announcer: Use repetition.
Boy: I'm hungry, hungry, hungry!
Announcer: Make an offer.
Boy: I'll be good. I promise.
Announcer: Add urgency.
Boy: I have to go potty!
Announcer: And presto! Your job is done. Let's try it: Step 1.
Boy: Mom!
Announcer: Step 2.
Boy: I want Pirro Brothers Pizza!
Announcer: Step 3.
Boy: Pirro Brothers! Pirro Brothers! Pirro Brothers!
Announcer: Step 4.

Boy: If you let me go to Pirro Brothers, I will stop making noises.
Announcer: Step 5.
Boy: Lalalalalala.
Announcer: A little more of Step 3.
Boy: I want Pirro Brothers! I want Pirro Brothers!
Announcer: And voila!
Mom: Okay!
Announcer: Dinner is served.
Boy: Yeaaaah!
Announcer: The next time you're hungry, try advertising.
Boy: I want Pirro Brothers!
Announcer: It works. Pirro Brothers Gourmet Pizza. In Woodstock on
                Route 47, next to Dollar Video. Pirro Brothers.
Boy: Are we there yet?

Turning the boy's hunger (a need) into mom's peace of mind (a want)

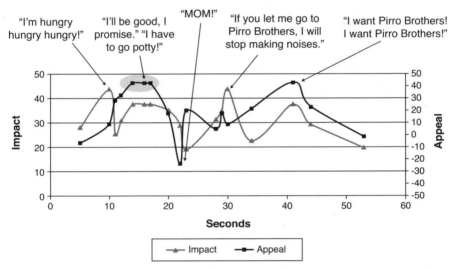

The easiest way to get to the 'me' in WIIFM is through emotions. Feelings don't have to break through the clutter; they're already inside us. How the boy in the Pirro Brothers Pizza radio spot feels is enough fuel by itself to turn a need into a want.

The outcome? The boy gets his pizza. But there's more to the story than that. The real plot revolves around needs and wants and the fuzzy line between them. Yes, the boy needs food. He wants pizza so badly, however, that this need crosses the line into becoming a want – evidence of emotion's power to escalate or otherwise transform our priorities. At the same time, the mother's preference for a little peace and quiet is so under siege from the boy's pleadings that it turns into a want, too. Only by succumbing to the boy's insistence can she achieve her goal: preserving her sanity!

Then there's the client. Pirro Brothers should be satisfied, too, as their brand name gets shouted out repeatedly at points in the spot's script that emotionally engage the people we tested.

Besides being consistently engaging and good at building the brand name into the script to create brand linkage, why else is this Pirro Brothers radio spot so great? For starters, it nicely illustrates a couple of important rules regarding motivations:

- First, motivations relate to survival instincts. To function most effectively and ward off threats, we focus first and foremost on what we feel will matter most (our needs).
- Second, we take action to change or regain the status quo. (The boy sought change: pizza. The mother sought to regain peace. Her choice about buying the pizza or not reflects the underlying psychological reality that ads address situations in which we seek either to resolve, evade or mitigate a situation the offer promises to address.)

The Pirro Brothers radio spot also relates well to the study of people's essential, universal motivations done by two psychologists at Harvard University: Paul Lawrence and Nitin Nohria. In *Driven: How Human Nature Shapes Our Choices*, they identify four core motivations (defend, acquire, learn and bond).[6] As a set, these four motivations provide a simple but comprehensive model for companies to use to, first, interpret and then strategically think (feel) through the motivations they want to leverage in their advertising campaigns.

Which of these motivations is relevant to the Pirro Brothers spot? In terms of what gets the highest impact scores, the focus shifts over the course of 60 seconds. At second 10, the initial peak comes when the boy says he's hungry (*defending* his ability to remain nourished). Then at second 30 the second peak in intensity happens when the boy raises the emotional ante. 'If you let me go to Pirro Brothers, I will stop making noises,' he says, thereby signalling that his *bond* with his mother might otherwise be sacrificed, so great is the allure of Pirro Brothers pizza.

BEING ON-MOTIVATION IS ESSENTIAL TO EFFECTIVENESS

In *What Sticks: Why Most Advertising Fails and How to Guarantee Yours Succeeds*, Rex Briggs and Greg Stuart look at ways in which they believe companies waste money. Based on their review of existing advertising campaigns, they conclude that 36 per cent of the marketers they studied didn't identify motivations effectively. In terms of US ad expenditures, the budget figure is over $50 billion misspent on that step alone – with another $35 billion wasted based on messaging that then becomes too fuzzy because the original motivation platform wasn't developed well.[7]

> *A problem–solution ad works if it's something relevant to me, even if the quality of the ad isn't great. I enjoy entertaining ads more but they don't usually convince me to buy a product.*
>
> Tony Hodgson, England

To test Briggs and Stuart's conclusion, I decided to use the most fully developed motivational model at my disposal. A few years before I discovered Lawrence and Nohria's model, I had worked with Andrew Ortony, a specialist in emotions at Northwestern University, to devise a set of 20 motivations divided into five groups of four motivations each. Next, my staff combed through our 10 years of project files to learn which of Ortony's five motivational categories get invoked most often in advertising and how effectively. Based on the facial-coding results, the outcomes are shown here:

Frequency and effectiveness of motivators in advertising

Motivation	Ad %	Engagement	% Positive	True Smile %
Physical	6%	36%	37%	1%
Empowerment	30%	43%	54%	8%
Attachment	10%	45%	83%	11%
Self-Esteem	16%	50%	49%	6%
Enjoyment	39%	37%	55%	11%

My favourite Dilbert cartoon is when he learns he's been assigned to marketing 'on a rotational basis'. Down the hallway he goes to his new job. Overhead is a banner: 'Welcome to Marketing, two drinks minimum'. Why mention that cartoon? Because as so often happens amid the chaos of marketing, people miss what's most important. Amid this small sea of numbers, what should stand out? It's that self-esteem is highest in engagement, and attachment highest in terms of positive emotional response created as a result of ads invoking that motivation. And yet, and yet... most ads focus on empowerment and enjoyment instead, which involve far less rich emotional pay dirt.

What does it all mean? Well, for one thing two groups of motivations – empowerment and enjoyment – predominate among the sampling we've tested. They're the most *prolific*. The second point, however, is that the self-esteem ads are the most emotionally *potent*. Half of the people we tested were engaged by them. Finally, the attachment group won handily in terms of the largest percentage of test participants whose overall emotional response was predominantly *positive* (while also tied for the most true-smile activity).

As a result of these emotional findings, it's my belief that a company's advertising will gain the most from focusing on self-esteem and attachment in terms of which motivations to leverage most.

Finally, as to tips on better plugging motivations into promoting an offer, how about asking the target market the open-ended question: 'Why might you start using this product?' Or show them a list of motivations and collect input about which one(s) the offer can plausibly address, and how well rivals are doing in that regard. No matter the approach, however, move beyond functional utility.

REDEFINING INDUSTRY CATEGORIES
AS EMOTIONAL MARKETS

As Gary Witt notes in *High Impact: How YOU Can Create Advertising That SELLS*, consumers don't trade their money for products so much as they're 'trading their money for satisfaction. In other words, they are trading their money for a feeling.'[8] But the *amount* of money we're willing to part with will vary, depending on whether a need, a want or a desire is involved.[9]

> *Very importantly, an ad should reach me at the right time when I am in need of a particular product. Otherwise, I will not change the brand I am already familiar with.*
>
> Kadulliah Ghazali, Malaysia

What's the difference between those three levels? A need is a must-have, a more or less logical, functional requirement that must be met by using, owning or experiencing the offer. A want is more like an expect-to-have, less logical, more emotional – a matter of benefits that we would like to have but don't truly require. (However, we fudge the line between needs and wants all the time in order to give ourselves an alibi for buying things we want but know are not related to basic, survival needs.) Finally, desires are the most emotional of the three types of positive motivations, a matter of daydreams.

They're the hope-to-haves. Desires are aspirational in nature and sometimes addressed by advertising headlines that use the word 'Be', ie become something that you're not right now.

Which type or level of motivation gets evoked depends, of course, on the nature of the offer and a company's strategy within a category. But there's also the particular marketplace and its relative degree of affluence. What many of my fellow Americans might have thought of as their bare-bones list of necessities during the Great Depression had, until the current Great Recession, been growing at an annual rate probably equivalent to their rising home values.

Meanwhile, in other countries with emerging economies, such as Vietnam, it's sobering to realize that the standard of living means that a motorbike, not a car, and an electric fan, not air conditioning, qualify as necessities. Meanwhile, a home computer isn't enough of a consideration to deserve a mention as one of the country's top 23 personal necessities (but a thick blanket does).[10]

The utter functionality of much of the Vietnamese list of necessities serves as a reminder of just how far Western societies have come in their lifestyles. In places like the United States, Japan, or in the most affluent of the European Union countries, many people have everything they realistically need. As a result, advertising plays a different role from that which it might in Vietnam – for instance, explaining why so-called First-World advertising is often no longer about explaining an offer's *functional* value so much as it is about telling a story about how the offer will enrich the *emotional* meaning of your life.[11]

As envisioned by Michael Silverstein, Neil Fiske and John Butman in *Trading Up*[12] and by Rolf Jensen in his groundbreaking book, *The Dream Society*,[13] in upscale target markets a person's basic needs have been met, commodities are everywhere, and fulfilling desires becomes the new, competitive frontier. The chart on page 96 is my synthesis of how the two books' respective models align, per market.

Often the types of offers per market create unusual bedfellows. For instance, in the affirmation market, financial services and consultants get lumped together with upscale ice cream because it can be seen as an indulgence, an act of self-pampering, to put so much of your key decision making into the hands of others. But don't let the apparent incongruities distract you. By seeing the category anew, with unexpected ties to other disparate parts of the economy, motivations can get tapped into from new angles. Then creative briefs can become more creative. And campaigns may improve their relevancy because, for campaigns to be on-emotion, they must also be strikingly on-motivation.

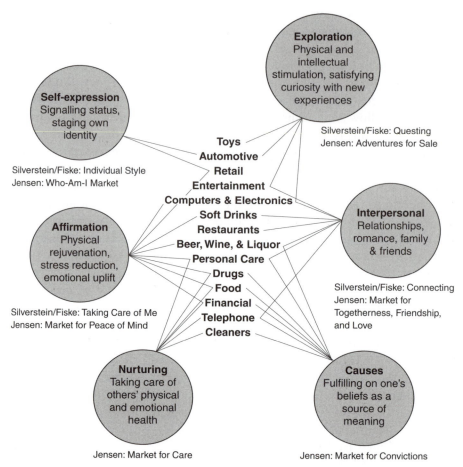

This chart shows the correlation between *Advertising Age*'s list of 14 top media spending categories and six different emotional markets. What's the point here? To get you to take your thinking beyond the commodity zone (of undifferentiated offer functionality) to tomorrow's more unique and lucrative emotional zone, where it's people's emotions and motivations – relevant to your offer – that should drive your advertising efforts, instead of the tired old features, attributes and benefits routine (so reflective of corporate inside-out thinking). Use the chart to rethink your category, and what it is that you are in essence providing to consumers. In that way, you can create new value and charge more, accordingly.

Two emotional markets, as depicted in advertising

The Bellwood ad addresses the market for care, urging people to realize that gambling is addictive and affects a person's mental health and social life as well as their wallet. On the right is an ad for Kohler, putting its faucets in the higher-end market for peace of mind by emphasizing the sense of flying above the ordinary that you'll enjoy.

RELEVANCY CREATED BY IDENTIFYING WITH THE EMOTIONS INVOLVED

Even when motivational relevancy isn't found in the offer, there are two other options to create more effective ads. Here I'll discuss the first option, which is to go directly to emotions themselves. By this I mean, an ad that can convincingly portray a universal, core emotion we've all experienced can in that way make itself *feel* relevant to the target market. Emotions are highly contagious. So this approach can work by leveraging the fact that each emotion comes with its own plot or meaning, as I am about to illustrate.

> *The key aspect to the execution is what emotional problem it is solving. Prior to execution we look at what the emotion is that we are trying to conquer.*
>
> Larry Kelley, creative director, FKM Agency

For instance, we may not think of ourselves as in the market for laundry detergent. We're not aware of being motivated to buy it. But everyone in life has felt disgust. So if an ad can convincingly portray being disgusted about dirty clothes, it has the possibility of influencing those who view it to emphasize or internalize that same emotion. What is the plot or meaning of disgust? As defined by psychologist Robert Plutchik,[14] disgust involves a judgment (this is poison), an action (to expel), a purpose (rejection), and an associated experience (disease or illness).

As a case in point, consider Procter & Gamble's 'Tide to Go' TV spot. In it, a job interviewee's attempt to land a new position (a highly relevant goal given the current economic downturn) is being undermined by an (animated) brown stain that literally talks over the poor guy. Not only does the stain drown out the applicant's would-be eloquence, the interviewer is distracted – and no doubt repulsed – by the brown mess with all its foul associations. If Tide can save the day, and the job, then clearly it's worth the purchase price.

Likewise, Plutchik has modelled the other core emotions as follows. Joy or happiness is about finding a mate or ally, wanting to 'possess' that person and reproduce because of desire. Surprise is about a gain or risk. It freezes you, while you orient to novelty. Moving on to negative emotions, fear involves danger, and escaping to protect oneself based on not wanting to experience death or loss; sadness involves a sense of abandonment, and seeking the support of others in order to cope; and finally, anger involves identifying an enemy, whom you want to attack and destroy, to overcome a barrier to progress.

Let me give two quick examples here of pertinent ads. For surprise, there's a Gatorade TV spot in which a lined foul ball heads for the corner of the baseball park. While the left fielder is comatose, the ball girl plays hero and stretches to make a leaping catch. The ball girl may be somewhat surprised by her miraculous catch, but we as viewers are even more so – and now long to become the sports heroes that we already are in our own fantasies (which Gatorade will presumably help make possible).

As to fear, Brink's Home Security has been running TV spots that take a woman-as-victim approach that has both raised sales (up 10 per cent in 2008) and led to blogosphere backlash. For instance, one blogger on the women-focused blog Jezebel has complained: 'We thank Brink's for the daily dose of irrational fear and for reminding us that as women we are vulnerable even when we're locked securely in our own homes.'[15]

Why are the Brink's TV spots at once so persuasive and offensive? That's because fear is a paralysing emotion, and so nobody who wants to feel either safe or empowered can tolerate it easily. Negative emotions, like fear, imply a threat, a risk. Survival is at stake. Like other negative emotions, it says to us, *I can be hurt*. So it's only natural that people gravitate to positive emotions, like hope, as quickly as possible to restore their comfort zone.

Taking this kind of emotional-relevancy analysis to its limits, across seven different advertising categories we've looked up which type of emotion gets invoked most often in people's experiencing of the ads we've tested. Here they are.

Emotion	Category of Most Common Occurrence
True Smile	Technology
Surprise	Retail
Sceptical	Technology
Dislike	Office
Sadness	Automotive
Frustration	Automotive
Anxiety	Alcohol

Hang in there with me on this one, because the chart needs some explaining. I'm *not* saying that surprise, for instance, is the single most common emotion that we show on our faces when we see a retail ad. Instead, what I *am* saying is that across seven industries, the category in which surprise is most common is retail. In other words, happiness may be more common as an emotional response to retail ads – but retail ads are unique in causing surprise most often of the seven categories we looked at.

Why do these results matter? That's because the emotions invoked are of use in interpreting your offer vis-à-vis the category it belongs to. Different categories have, as we found, different emotions that they uniquely inspire most strongly in us. Sometimes it's good news: an emotion you will want to leverage in your advertising. Other times, it's bad news but, hey, deal with it; it's reality: an emotion that exists in people's hearts that you'll need to deflect or otherwise mitigate.

As for the results themselves, there are some interesting combinations. For instance, technology-related ads generate not only the most true-smile enjoyment but also the most scepticism (smiles combined with negative, doubting verbal reactions). So it's a split verdict there. How about the automotive category? Maybe the often too technical nature of the ads not only frustrates us, it also leaves us feeling down (as we struggle to understand).

What's the single most intriguing combination? That award goes to alcohol, with at once both the most anxiety and the most happiness overall (55 per cent of the facial muscle activity is smiles, though only 4 per cent true smiles). Do we feel anxious about enjoying our booze so much? Or drinking to mask pain? In comparison, the most straightforward signature responses belong, first, to retailer ads that create curiosity (surprise); and second, to advertising related to office products which, given work associations, quite naturally generate the largest amount of dislike (a mixture of disgust and contempt).

Now, tell that little titbit to your boss next Monday!

RELEVANCY CREATED BY IDENTIFYING WITH A BRAND'S PERSONALITY TYPE

Moving on from emotions, a second angle to generate indirect, non-motivational relevancy is advertising that leverages a brand's innate personality type. Out ahead in this regard are Margaret Mark and Carol Pearson. In *The Hero and the Outlaw: Building Extraordinary Brands Through the Power of Archetypes*, they identify 12 character types familiar to us based on folk tales, mythology and movies, among other sources.[16]

Rooted as Mark and Pearson's approach is in figures drawn from common sources, they offer something almost everyone can relate to easily. And therein lies the advantage to advertising of using personality types as an alternative means of generating motivational relevancy. After all, who among us hasn't at various stages or moments in life felt like we could relate to, or be enacting, any one of these 12 roles in our own lives? Maybe even more to the point here, don't most of us have an underlying emotional disposition or outlook on life that causes us to gravitate to playing outlaw or jester, for instance? I think we do.

Taking on industry categories again, here are some instinctive ways I might link companies and archetypal characters. Using three categories as examples, here's a list of some possible fits.

Typecasting deluxe: industry categories and brand profiles within them

Automotive

Company	Archetype	Reason
General Motors	(fading) Ruler	Was on top, trying to rebound
Toyota	Magician	Pushing to create Green vehicles
Ford	Regular Guy/Gal	How pick-up drivers see selves
Hyundai	Caregiver	Lets you return car if you lose job
BMW	Sage	Superior knowledge

Personal care

Company	Archetype	Reason
Dove	Regular Guy/Gal	Real models people can relate to
Gillette	Hero	Studly guys ready for action
Neutrogena	Innocent	Soft milky tones, offering trust
Olay	Ruler & Creator	Take control of your aging theme
Garnier	Jester & Explorer	Talent with huge smiles; fruity, bright brand colours – excitement

Restaurants

Company	Archetype	Reason
McDonald's	Caregiver/Innocent	Family focused, 'happy meals'
Burger King	Jester & Explorer	Being positioned as The Rolling Stones of the category
Subway	Creator & Hero	Looking to be fresh, protect you
Starbucks	Sage	A brand for connoisseurs
Applebee's	Regular Guy/Gal	Midwest brand for mid-America

Every category seems to have a leading brand that most naturally fits the Regular Guy/Gal characterization. Otherwise, the personality positionings shown here vary widely, giving the brands a chance to separate – and distinguish – their brand from those of rivals. Can you say the same of your brand? What is its archetypal identity, and is it different enough from those of competitors within your industry category that it helps you create both an emotional bond with your target market *and* a sense of uniqueness?

As Mark and Pearson suggest, per category a company should think about how it can differentiate itself through a projected personality type. But obviously in doing so, a company should strategically consider its target market and define a personality that's salient, acceptable and/or aspirational for the consumers meant to support the brand. For instance, John McEnroe is often a great commentator at Wimbledon. But as a celebrity spokesperson, he's clearly an outlaw – which leaves me to wonder what standards of decorum National Car Rental seeks to violate in using him in its advertising?

SUMMARY

Companies can take either a direct or an indirect approach to boosting the relevancy of their marketing. For instance, in *Gimme!*, John Hallward reports that the more emotional drivers (motivations) that get invoked by an ad, the greater the purchase intent. But Hallward also reports that nearly 50 per cent of persuasion is based on better emotional brand associations, such as creating an appealing personality.[17] So there's clearly more than one way to enact the rule that relevancy drives connection (and consideration of a company's offer).

When all is said and done, relevancy has to do with possibilities. A company's advertising must show a willingness to acknowledge, and address, our unspoken questions: 'Why should I care about what you're telling me? How will my life be better with your help?' A company that can make us *feel* like it understands our problems creates affinity and opportunities to sell-in.

Takeaways include:

- We take action to change or regain the status quo. Ads address situations in which we seek to resolve, evade or mitigate a situation the offer promises to sort out. Our emotions turn on when one of our needs, wants, desires or fears is at stake.
- Creativity in an advertising context might wisely be redefined as the creation of emotions in us that promote consideration rather than rejection of an advertised offer. The problem must be made vivid enough for us to be drawn in and ready to accept the offer's value.
- One model involves the four core motivations of defend, acquire, learn and bond, in relation to which the offer can be strategically positioned.
- Another model involves five motivational groupings: physical, empowerment, attachment, self-esteem and enjoyment. Our emotional research results indicate that self-esteem and attachment are, respectively, the most engaging and positive in nature.
- In an era of commoditization, industry categories can be redefined as emotional markets. Six possibilities are self-expression, affirmation, nurturing, exploration, interpersonal and causes.
- Two other non-motivational routes to establishing relevancy are to invoke one of the universal core emotions or any of a dozen archetypal characters to create a brand personality that will resonate with consumers.

7

Always sell hope

ORIENTATION

The essence of advertising is to promote positive feelings. Sometimes, the advertising can do so in and of itself, through the use of humour, music and dramatic effects. But to ensure revenue, the key is to invoke the advertised brand offer as the ultimate solution to our enduring desire for something big, new and positive.

Put another way, it's the promise of new, enhanced possibilities that we long for. It's the heart fighting through the scepticism of the media-savvy 21st-century mind. In 1980, Al Ries and Jack Trout could still dare to write in *Positioning* that a primary goal of advertising 'is to heighten expectations. To create the *illusion* that the product or service will perform the *miracles* you expect.'[1] But now scepticism is like a disease that's reached an advanced state. So to protect integrity (or at least perceptions of it), a company should, in my opinion, conduct claims-versus-reality testing of the kind that will be examined at the end of this chapter.

HAPPINESS, INC.: LEVERAGING THE HOPE THAT SPRINGS ETERNAL

Hope that promises happiness isn't trivial. Hope as the harbinger of happiness is vital because 'Happiness brings vitality' quite literally. When we become happy, our bodies experience change. Not only does our blood pulse an extra three to five heartbeats a minute, but our skin temperature also warms by about a tenth of a degree Centigrade and parts of our brain light up as well.[2]

Happiness, Inc.: an advertising staple

Smiling, happy, satisfied customers: it's an advertising staple. What's almost as common? The yellow smiley that sometimes appears in ads and was also the face that Walmart used to have on its employees' vests before it encountered legal issues involving the smiley face's creator, Harvey Ball.

As neurobiologists and psychologists have learned, happiness delivers all sorts of benefits:

- Physically – positive feelings counteract stress; muscles relax, making us more flexible and agile.
- Socially – happier people are nicer, more aware, better able to navigate conflicts with others.
- Intellectually – being happier makes us more creative, better able to solve problems and do so quickly. In a way, being generally happy can make us *smarter*. Positive feelings make it easier for the brain to make new mental connections because the brain gets flooded with the enablers of serotonin and dopamine. More specifically, researcher Mark Jung-Beeman has shown that people in good moods do significantly better at solving hard problems than people who are downbeat – by a margin of nearly 20 per cent.[3]

I definitely pay attention to ads that are positive and provide hope. Negative advertising does not work for me. I think ads lose their purpose if they are negative.

Kersti Oja Kringlie, United States

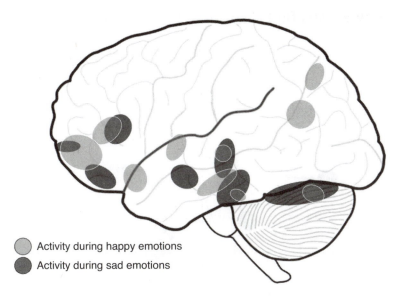

Activity during happy emotions
Activity during sad emotions

fMRI brain scans are now beginning to identify which parts of the brain 'light up' when certain emotions are felt. As is true of facial coding, it's interesting how often the two emotions are physically adjacent or overlapping, as if sadness is the back side of the shining moon of happiness.

So there's a scientific basis to my advice to always sell hope. The research verdict is that 'Reward and pleasure are always better motivators than force and fear of punishment.'[4] But how well do companies promote pleasure in their advertising? To find out, Morris Holbrook and Rajeev Batra had a team of independent adult judges watch, in total, 72 commercials that had recently run during national prime-time television. The team of 60 judges was then asked to rate the spots, including on the two emotional dimensions of appeal and enthusiasm.[5]

The team's rational results are shown here (page 106) in contrast to my staff checking the files for the emotional results to advertising we've tested in the same six industry categories, likewise using our appeal scores but substituting impact for enthusiasm.

As you can see, the study's judges weren't happy campers about what they saw in the TV spots. Half of the six categories landed in negative-appeal territory in their case, indicating a lack of pleasure. Meanwhile, our facial-coding results show far greater promise in terms of advertising's ability to deliver both hope and happiness. Every category is in our results in positive-appeal territory, and in three cases (food, technology and health) the level of impact (or enthusiasm) is notably higher, too.

Think versus feel responses to category advertising

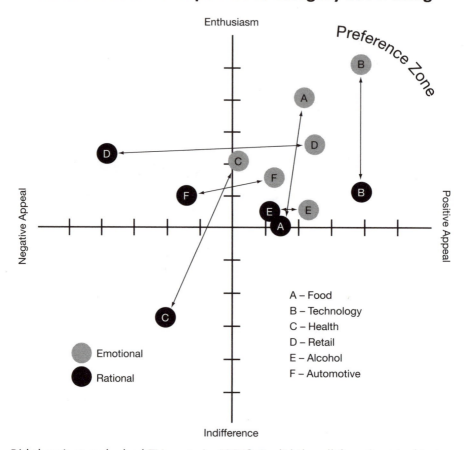

A – Food
B – Technology
C – Health
D – Retail
E – Alcohol
F – Automotive

Emotional

Rational

Did they just make bad TV spots in 1987? Or did the all-female set of judges living in the vicinity of Columbia University and characterized by a 'serious demeanour' just not like the commercials they were given to evaluate? (Maybe their evaluations actually reflect a New Yorker's view of TV spots aimed at mid-America!) Who can say. What's obvious, however, is that in this case the facial-coding results are far more positive. Yes, the two sets of results fall into more or less the same ranking, based on appeal. But our results are more upbeat, with much higher points on the axis defined as impact (or enthusiasm).

Encouraging news? Yes. But for all companies in all categories to do consistently well at promoting positive feelings in us, it's worthwhile to better understand our criteria for happiness and the role that hope plays in creating it. In short, what *specifically* makes people happy? To improve your advertising, read on.

THE INTERRELATED DYNAMICS OF HAPPINESS AND HOPE: AN ADVERTISER'S CHECKLIST

While there are many experts on happiness, I'm going to limit my focus to two of them. The first is Marty Seligman, who in 1998 launched the positive psychology movement with his equation: $H = S + C + V$ (Happiness equals our genetic Set point, plus Circumstances, plus what we Voluntarily change). Granted, there's not much we – or advertisers – can do about inherited genetics, one's natural physical and mental disposition or 'set point'. But *circumstances* can certainly include favourable exposure to advertising – and provide an opportunity for companies to alter the left side of the equation by changing feelings for the better.

The other expert is Stefan Klein, author of the international bestseller, *The Science of Happiness*. Distilling the essence of the two men's conclusions about what causes happiness results in what could be thought of as a bullseye image.

Compared with the outer rings, what's the core of happiness?[6,7,8] It's not fleeting pleasures of the flesh (or bottle). Those are the weakest, least valuable outer ring of the bullseye. Nor is it the mentally active version of seeking variety and novelty (engagement). That's the next, more inner ring. Instead, the enduring, inner circle of happiness consists of meaningfulness, caused by two factors. The first is the warmth and depth of our ties to other people. The second is feeling hopeful instead of helpless about our circumstances, because we control them and/or are part of a society where people largely play by the rules.

Put another way, happiness has three sources of ever-greater importance the more you move toward the circle's centre. Physical pleasures and being mentally and spiritually engaged contribute to happiness. Companies that advertise offers aimed at either the source of the outer or middle circle of happiness definitely have a basis to operate from, but the emotional pay-off won't be as rich.

Speaking of 'richness', what's missing here (you may say) is another variable: wealth and material comfort. Granted, incomes across much of the world have grown substantially over the past half-century. But the percentage of people describing themselves as happy hasn't actually changed all that much. As it turns out, a comfortable, even luxurious, lifestyle can help but doesn't guarantee happiness in and of itself.[9]

Indeed, returning to the feeling hopeful, versus helpless, element that's part of happiness's core, a major factor in whether people in wealthy or poor countries consider themselves happy is the degree of corruption plaguing their society.[10] In mentioning corruption, have I gone off track? Not much. For in alluding to the uncertainty of justice in lawless places, my real point here is to now bring hope into the equation.

So far I have been talking about happiness. But what's the relationship between happiness and hope, and how can understanding that dynamic be of benefit to companies wanting to ensure that their advertising has greater emotional voltage? Here's how.

Happiness and hope are intimately linked. It doesn't matter which psychology model you look at. In every case, the two emotions stand cheek to jowl. That's because while joy (the highest level of happiness, and the equivalent of a true smile) is about being pleased with an event, hope is about being pleased by the prospect of a desirable event. In other words, happiness (joy) is present tense; hope is future tense. But of the two, hope is, indeed, fundamentally *tense*.

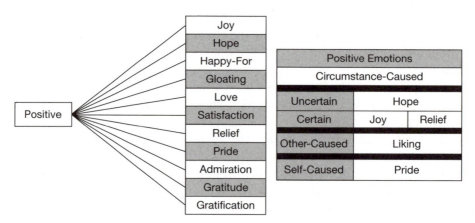

In the middle is a ranking of positive emotions, from the most positive to least among them. Notice how joy and hope occupy the adjacent top two rungs. Meanwhile, to the right is a diagram that shows five of those positive emotions. Notice that the difference between joy and hope isn't just a matter of happiness achieved or in waiting; it's also that hope is *uncertain*. The expectation of it both tantalizes and leaves us worried it won't happen, hence the cliché about 'hoping against hope'.

What I mean is that in always selling hope, companies must recognize that hope involves trust. As hopeful consumers, we believe in the expectation of fulfilment. We're optimistic. We're encouraged. We anticipate being happy – but in evaluating a company's advertising in our heart of hearts, we're also afraid we won't be in the end. *And that's where my apparent digression about corruption enters the picture.*

> *I'm all about hope. Hope is a wonderful thing. I'm not going to give into fear. Ads that have a guy pulling a girl out of a car crash, and saying that you are glad you have this type of insurance are ridiculous and I do not buy into them.*
>
> Jean-Charles David, France

As consumers, we don't control the quality of the offers we purchase. We might haggle about the price, but there again we don't typically have much influence now that the mom-and-pop shops are no longer so common. Advertising, however, is something we have a lot of say about. It's up to us to decide whether we turn it off or turn away from it, and the company whose advertising feels *emotionally corrupt* because it sells hope wantonly, without regard for the truth, without regard to it feeling like plausible hope, is in trouble.

That kind of company will start by depriving us of happiness based on our experiences of the offer post-purchase. But that same company will also ultimately no longer be in the business of selling hope because the uncertainty of what we'll get after we buy grows too large and snuffs out the hope that advertising depends on for its very effectiveness.

Put another way, hope is guarded. It's emotionally rich, but tense – as it involves fearing the worst but wanting better. Advertising that doesn't silence the fears of disappointment or, in fact, inadvertently creates doubt and fear, is no longer promoting desire. It's no wonder that hope sits second from the top of the ladder of positive feelings, so great a force is anticipation. But in their hopes of selling hope, some companies are better at it than others. Pitfalls await, as we're about to see.

A CRITIQUE OF THREE EXAMPLES
OF SELLING BOTH HOPE AND HAPPINESS

Just as not all causes of happiness are of equal importance, so it's likewise true that in advertising not all executions striving to promote hope and happiness do equally well. Here are three examples, of which the first two are drawn from my company's project files as quantifiable evidence that climbing up to the top rungs of the positive-feelings ladder isn't so easily done.

Example 1: Open-road happiness

One of our first projects was for a large do-it-yourself, truck-rental moving company. Among nine different versions of signage, meant to attract more customers, three options that were based on rational ratings looked equally promising. The first option, A, showed the trucks you'd use for moving your things. The second option, B, showed the usual rental price, and the third option, C, showed a curving open road.

Loading up, paying up or hitting the open road: what's best?

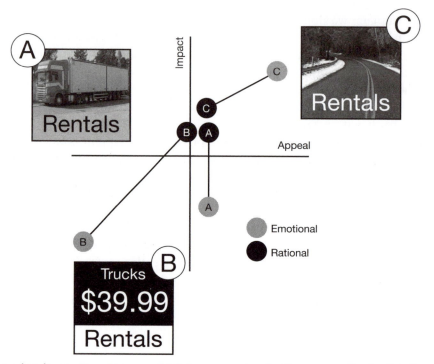

I used to live in New Jersey, which has more trucks than cows. So don't tell me that Option A is attractive signage. As to Option B, well, as Chapter 8 will discuss, seeing price tags tends to arouse disgust in most of us. That leaves Option C, the open road, reminiscent of a great old Animals song, *We Got to Get Out of This Place (If It's the Last Thing We Ever Do)*. Now who hasn't had that feeling about a job, apartment or relationship?

Emotionally, however, the results look very different. Both options A and B fall away, which makes gut-level sense. Trucks are hardly sexy vehicles, compared with driving a Ferrari or BMW. What's to be hopeful about? Rental trucks are, instead, more like beasts of burden as you prepare to haul your own stuff to another town. As for B, who among us would believe that's the complete cost? (Aren't there various taxes and hidden fees to consider?) Remember that hopes that won't be dashed and ultimately abandoned involve trust. Besides, over time the price will go up – forcing the company to replace all the existing signage!

That leaves option C. It's poetry. It's Walt Whitman's 'Song of the Open Road' delivered visually. It plays to the Americana theme of 'Go west, young man (and woman).' Find yourself. Explore. As such, it's no surprise that emotionally C ran away with the prize. It delivers on the key criteria for both hope and happiness.

Let me explain. In regards to hope, it's perfect because it promises you only what the open road promises you: nothing but a chance for expectations to be fulfilled. Meanwhile, in regards to happiness, the open-road signage is likewise great because inactivity (physical and mental) along with a sense of helplessness comprise the two greatest threats to happiness. Here the open road provides, instead, the opportunity to seize on variety and novelty, as happens when you're starting life anew.

Example 2: Unconventional independence

A direct-mail piece we tested for a major insurance company did a good job delivering emotionally on a different source of happiness. In this case, the source was the perennial human desire for security and order (controlling one's circumstances to avoid feeling helpless – and hopelessly lost).

On the front side of this self-mailer, a little girl is shown holding a garden hose. Behind her sits a shiny red convertible, top down, seats filled with water. Little yellow plastic duckies and beach balls float on the inland sea that she has created in her parents' driveway, inside the car. Not only did the target market of drivers with problematic records like it on exposure (the percentage of positive feelings it generated came in 20 per cent above our norms), but the company later confided that no direct-mail piece in its history had ever generated such a large response.

Why? Well, in regards to hope, if the little girl's 'vandalism' is as bad as it gets, life is still pretty good. Eagerness for enjoying life remains intact. Meanwhile, in regards to happiness, the girl's cute. It's an empathetic pleasure to see her enjoying herself, and the whole scene with the little girl and the pleasant home speaks to being socially rooted.

> *You do not build anything with fear. Hope is a source of help. During the occupation times in Estonia, we muted out the sound during commercials because the fear factor was so strong. It's a complete turn-off for Estonians now. Estonian ads are very straight to the point, short, sweet, and factual.*
>
> Katrin Nogols, Estonia

Example 3: Great brands feel alike

Let's now move, in greater depth, across advertising media and around the world. As the current Great Recession began to take its emotional toll on us in late 2008 and early 2009, Pepsi and Coca-Cola more or less simultaneously launched their own versions of happiness ad campaigns.

Pepsi came first, with cans and bottles showing a new smiling logo. The turning of the white portion of its old logo, sideways, to resemble a smile, didn't make media critics happy, however. Its extension into a print-ad execution led David Kiley of *Businessweek* to lampoon it as a 'rip-off' of Barack Obama's campaign iconography.[11] But Pepsi wasn't about to stop. It celebrated New Year's Eve, 2009, with a Times Square billboard using the Pepsi logo as a lit-up 'o' in words like 'optimism', 'wow', 'joy' and 'love'. (I guess adding 'hope' to that list would have been simply too obviously derivative of Obama!)

Shortly thereafter, Coke launched the 'Open Happiness' campaign that had apparently been in the works for a year. A global campaign included a billboard in which opened bottle caps – shaped like Os – float like bubbles in the air.

'It's really about those timeless values of optimism, what makes people happy,' said Katie Bayne, Coke's North America chief marketing officer in an article appearing in *The Atlanta Journal-Constitution*. 'It's really a statement about the little, simple joys,' said Joe Tripoldi, Coke's chief marketing officer. 'We represent a small moment or small pleasure in a sometimes very stressful or difficult day for people,' he added.[12]

Regarding the ability of 'Open Happiness' to speak to consumers 'who are financially and emotionally distressed by the recession', mediabistro.com says it's a 'tall order coming from a can of pop'.

Bingo. That's exactly right, and it's the problem here with both campaigns. As acknowledged by one and all here, the kind of happiness a carbonated beverage can bring us fits the least substantial cause of happiness: sensory pleasure. The fulfilment we will be hoping for is slight. But the degree and global-wide amount of plagiarism are great. Whether it's ripping off Obama or seemingly each other, it's all reminiscent of a favourite rhyming couplet of Wall Street's: 'God gave us eyes: plagiarize.' There can be little hope of happiness's deepest source, meaningfulness, when neither brand comes across to us as worthy of a unique, committed relationship.

BEHAVIOURAL ECONOMICS AND THE TENSION BETWEEN HOPE AND FEAR IN ADVERTISING

During most of the 20th century, economists effectively banned emotions. In their hard-nosed world, desire disappeared in favour of utility: making decisions to maximize gain. But supported by the breakthroughs in brain science that affirm the central role of emotions in decision making, a new breed of economists, behavioural economists, are now providing insights marketers would be wise to explore.

In essence, what behavioural economists point out is that people are overly optimistic and, therefore, not nearly objective enough to enact the kind of self-disciplined utility maximization that traditional economists espouse as their model. Put another way, behavioural economists accept the influence of blind faith and crippling fear alike. They're okay with the idea that consumers are, quite simply, people, not robots. That we're collectively less like Mr Spock from *Star Trek* and more like Homer Simpson from *The Simpsons*.

Why does that matter to advertisers?

The explanation is that in seeking to maintain hope and gain happiness, we're our own spin doctors. As scientists have noted, 'people go to great lengths to view the world in a way that maintains a sense of well-being'.[13] Hope and happiness are fragile.

So in a mental battle between preserving hope versus taking an accurate look at our motivations, most times it's easy to predict the outcome. We choose psychological immunity. We protect ourselves from bad news, which means that advertising works more effectively when it takes into account our natural tendency to treat on-message 'facts' as either malleable or irrelevant.

In other words, what matters instead is how an ad makes us *feel*. With that in mind, let's look at my distillation of behavioural economics into seven key principles about human nature that advertising should never, ever, lose sight of.

Principle 1: Loss aversion

Nothing is more crucial here than the reality that for most of us losses don't feel the same as gains. In fact, research indicates that losses loom larger in our psyches by a ratio of about two to one. For instance, professional money managers have been shown to hold losing stocks twice as long as they do their better stocks, costing them probably something on the order of 3.4 per cent of their portfolio return. Nevertheless, behaviour like that happens because people try to postpone pain, leading to more losses than would be rationally expected.[14]

Fear of regret, and fear in general, is the key emotion and motivation here.

Advertising application: By showing babies comfortably engaged in transactions online, E-Trade is memorably making the point that trading and banking online are so easy a six-month-old can do them. Fear shouldn't be a factor, nor therefore should a need to handle your investments in the same way your dad did. In perhaps the best TV spot, the baby is interrupted in the middle of doing some business online by a call from his girlfriend.

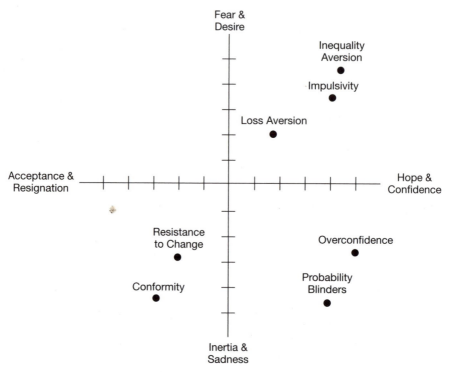

This chart tries to help you out, dear reader, by diagramming where the seven principles I'm about to discuss fall in terms of energy level (the north–south axis) or being positively oriented (the east–west axis). In the end, it's really about the emotional mind games we play with ourselves in order to preserve (irrational) hope while also keeping fear at bay. Las Vegas casinos, state lotteries, dieting plans and the purchase of soon-to-be-neglected exercise equipment are among the examples. Of them, the exercise equipment is actually my favourite: a case where buyers blame themselves when they don't work out, while the seller's profit remains intact.

Principle 2: Resistance to change

As everybody knows, people procrastinate. We deny knowing what we know, including the need to adapt. Perhaps the actor John Belushi's best line ever was when he was playing Congressman Sam Irwin of Watergate fame and asked the question 'What I want to know is, what did the President know and when did he stop knowing it?'

Sloth is a key motivation here, aided by complacency and a bias in favour of what's familiar.

Advertising application: A TV spot by Monster, the internet job want-ads option, shows a stork braving the elements to deliver a baby boy. Jump ahead 30 years: the child is a drone stuck in a dead-end job. The message of 'Are you reaching your potential?' is a call to action for a target market that might otherwise be more inclined to indulge inertia and stick with the status quo.

> *By carefully framing an alternative so that it appears far more attractive than it really is, marketers can increase sales, increase profits and create extraordinary loyalty to products and services that perform no better, or even worse, than far less expensive competitive offerings.*
>
> Gary Stibel, founder and CEO, New England Consulting

Principle 3: Conformity

We go against our own instincts in order to conform to the social status quo. In reality, we don't always weigh the alternatives much, if at all, because we find it easier to simply accept the consensus choices of others. The cliché that 'Nobody ever got fired for choosing IBM' explains the motivation here as well as anything else: self-preservation based on the philosophy that going along is getting along (with people).

Think of it as peer pressure, being intimidated into cautious behaviour.

Advertising application: A TV spot for Miller High Life shows one of their delivery men in a baseball skybox, incredulous – and appalled – by the surrounding group of cheese-nibbling elites who aren't even watching the game. In disavowing the group he's with, the delivery man is actually at the same time avowing his allegiance to (and conformity with) a larger group of down-to-earth beer drinkers, a target market big enough to make the sponsor lots of money.

Principle 4: Probability blinders

According to traditional economics, we have a pretty good understanding of the probabilities and consequences of each possible course of action. Get real! For reasons ranging from lack of sleep to lack of time, knowledge or basic smarts, we often have a hard time processing new information and making judgments based on it. To cope with too much information, we often seize on minor details, distorting how we frame our decisions.

The key motivation is an unerring (but not always bad) instinct to go with what we feel in our gut, thereby loading the dice in favour of a decision we've already subconsciously made – facts be damned!

Advertising application: In Vietnam, a person put out an ad letting people know that his house has a swallow's nest, which in that country is considered a sign of good luck that will bring prosperity. The house sold immediately. A Vietnamese real-estate agency named Salangane has now incorporated this approach into its latest advertising campaign.

Principle 5: Overconfidence

We're forever overestimating our own abilities and the likelihood of positive outcomes. We're aided in this bias by a tendency to be selective about what we remember or choose to focus on. In basic terms, it's a matter of ego and wanting to feel good about ourselves as well as impress, influence and win over others.

Pride is the key emotion and motivator here.

Advertising application: In Canada, the Mini Cooper's ad agency has run some (politically) cheeky billboards. The one that showed the car along with the words, 'We're not saying we're better than SUVs. Al Gore is,' plays on people's delight in feeling superior to others based on being able to make the right purchase decisions.

Principle 6: Impulsivity

Think of it as lust, as greed, the chasing down of often oversized expectations. In short, desire transforms us. We discount risks we should take seriously and justify our actions by 'proof' that comes easily to mind.

Oscar Wilde's quip, 'I can resist everything except temptation,' summarizes this principle.

Advertising application: A TV spot by Captain Morgan, in which a guy gets a text message from some friends in a nearby bar. The image of the friends with three hotties is promising. When he rushes to O'Reilly's, however, the reality is that his 'friends' only want a designated driver. The spot has dramatic tension because we don't know if he'll be amused or angry as he learns the news that he is expected to find abstinence a virtue.

Principle 7: Inequality aversion

Research shows that our instinct for wanting fairness and justice is incredibly strong and can override all other considerations. For instance, we will harm our own self-interests and break off an otherwise good deal in order to avoid letting somebody else get the better of us in negotiations.

Feelings like outrage and vengeance are relevant here, while the motivations vary from altruism (let's all play fair and be nice) to injured self-esteem ('I'm no less important than you are!').

Advertising application: In France, airline Transavia has been running ads that tell people to hurry up and buy a plane ticket before all the big bankers take every seat in their rush to abandon the country. The approach is appealing twice over: save some money and deprive the bankers of getting the inside track on things (for once). The underlying message: Exact revenge; you may be worth less, but you're more worthy than the bankers are.

THE MISSING FACTOR IN SELLING HOPE: BE TRUE TO YOUR WORD(S)

To reiterate: it feels good to feel good. As cited earlier, there are basic survival advantages to being happy. It lifts our energy level, our ability to solve problems and to attract allies, as evidenced by the saying, 'Nobody knows you when you're down and out.' As a result, behavioural economics is very much on track in recognizing that we're naturally our own spin doctors, often happily caught up in a web of self-deception.

But when do companies run foul of the way we will instinctively seek to avoid taking a hard look at things? When they fail to acknowledge – and honour – another key rule that involves hope: the rule of reciprocity. In other words, when do we focus with laser-like emotionally charged clarity? When we don't feel like we're getting what we expected, wanted – and *deserve* – from the other party.

> *I pay attention to adverts that are authentic. Adverts that provide a sense of false hope, eg 'Feed the hungry,' are a big turn-off for me. However, if an advert delivers real hope and engages me emotively, I notice it.*
>
> Sacha du Plessis, South Africa

Let me explain by telling a quick story. Years ago, I was finishing up my research presentation involving a major new international launch for a big pharmaceutical company. The results weren't as good as everyone would have liked, but there was general agreement with my assessment of why the engagement level and amount of positive emotional responses from the study participants had been low. One person from the company then voiced the problem, suddenly declaring: 'Yep, we're very good at figuring out what's in it for us. But we're not *nearly* so good at figuring out what's in it for the end user.'

It was an incisive comment, reflecting a reality that goes well beyond that particular company and a single launch.

Remember that the last of the seven principles of behavioural economics that I just introduced is inequality aversion. We have a keen sensitivity to justice. Companies that don't practise reciprocity destroy the hope they seek to instil in prospective customers. Because survival is really the bottom line, and somebody who doesn't prove to be your ally is, instead, merely a parasite, it makes sense that in the end the strongest influence on brand equity is product performance.[15]

Hope fulfilled trumps mere promises, every time. Therefore, companies should strive to take two steps that will protect the viability of their advertising long term. Selling false hope might possibly work for a while but, ultimately, real reciprocity wins. Historically true because the press might pick up on customer dissatisfaction and run an expose about it, the downside of not giving people what they pay for and expect is even more of a problem nowadays given the role of social media. Suddenly, what was a matter of (bad) word-of-mouth advertising, practised among neighbours and friends, can, thanks to Twitter, Facebook and the like, be digitally shared around the world. As companies have sometimes painfully learned, viral reactions to corporate shams and misdeeds quickly take on a life of their own.

The first step is obvious: focus on end-user benefits. Don't get caught up in the offer-as-hero syndrome that can happen only too easily because:

- It's easier to get the client, the company, to sign off on creative in which the offer is front and centre, as hero, bolstering the corporate ego.
- Contrary to the keep it simple rule, the assumption is made that we will look at the features and attributes being touted and figure out the benefits for ourselves.
- Playing it safe, the corporate lawyers won't allow the company to advertise any specific benefits in case they get viewed as false promises.[16]

Meanwhile, the second step – best enacted as a baseline test prior to every campaign that introduces new, explicit or implicit claims related to a product or service – is what a client of mine once asked for. The authors of *The Little Blue Book of Advertising* advocate running what they call 'promise tests' that don't test concepts or executions but, rather, identify which benefits might resonate best with the target market. In this case, my client went even further. First, we tested how consumers experienced the product – and then how well the advertising reflected the reality of the product's features and benefits.

The purpose: to protect the trust on which hope depends long term.
Clearly, test participants weren't reassured by what this spot conveyed, and that's a shame. As this promise test discovered, the target market actually liked the new product a lot. In fact, test subjects' emotional response to the

Spot is weaker than product

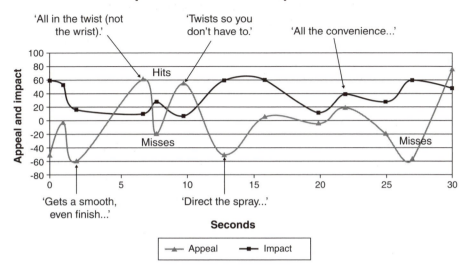

'All in the twist (not the wrist).'

'Twists so you don't have to.'

'All the convenience...'

Hits

Misses

Misses

Appeal and impact

Seconds

'Gets a smooth, even finish...'

'Direct the spray...'

Appeal   Impact

new offer itself was 31 per cent more positive than it was on average for the three radio spots we tested for the client. Talk about a wasted opportunity!

SUMMARY

Selling hope, the promise of happiness, underlies marketing. Do it well and faithfully, and the advertising can work as many miracles as a good offer will support. Promise testing – whether of benefits to be showcased in the advertising or of the claimed benefits vis-à-vis the target market's actual offer experience – should be used to ensure that the hopes being promoted are grounded in reality. Otherwise, without verification, without proof, companies run a huge risk of selling false, unsubstantiated hope and getting harmed commercially not only through negative word of mouth but also, these days, by getting 'flamed' by negative feedback posted on the internet.

Some things in business are mighty complicated, but this one isn't: hope that translates into true satisfaction leads to yet another key business metric: feelings of loyalty.

Takeaways include:

- The essence of advertising is to promote positive feelings. Two emotions are the key here: happiness and hope.
- Happiness delivers all sorts of benefits, from greater physical agility to more social grace and intellectual creativity. As an emotion, it's rooted

in enjoying physical pleasure, intellectual exploration, and the meaning-fulness that comes from belonging and a sense of security and order.

- Hope is more guarded. It involves fearing the worst but wanting better and therefore inherently involves a degree of tension and apprehension. Advertising that doesn't silence the fears of disappointment will inadvert-ently create doubt and fear instead.
- The seven principles of behavioural economics give marketers insights regarding how to frame choices in ways that will play to people's emotional manipulating of reality.
- Because hope involves trusting that something good will come of the advertised offer, companies that only make promises they won't fulfil are violating the fundamental rule of emotional reciprocity, ie consumers look to get what they expect for their money.

8

Don't lead with price

ORIENTATION

As I write this book, the global economy is in the midst – or perhaps near the bottom – of the worst downturn in half a century. Today's Great Recession has adversely affected media spending, of course. But I'm about to argue that it can also harm advertising's emotional depth. Ad after ad on TV, in print, on radio, etc is currently emphasizing 'value' or 'promotion' as a code for 'low price' or 'bargain' or 'discount', inviting contempt from consumers who may see the offer as merely cheap.

CHEAPO-NOMICS:
AN EXAMPLE OF 'VALUE' ADVERTISING IN PRACTICE

Why companies are now leading with price in advertising is obvious. As strapped for cash as their suddenly frugal customers, companies are understandably choosing to run sales and promotions that can bring in some revenue. I get it; I run a company myself, after all. Covering operating expenses while trying to make a living is a valid goal. Longer term, however, advertising that leads with price can hurt more than it helps for seven emotional reasons that I'll cover before ending this chapter with other, better ways to handle the value = quality/price equation.

HOW LEADING WITH PRICE
CAN DESTROY A COMPANY'S MARKETING STRATEGY

Yes, there are financial arguments against leading with price. None is more basic than the fact that by definition only one offer per category can be the lowest cost at any moment in time – leading to a brutal game of operational efficiency and/or attrition. The ease with which we can price-compare on the internet only makes the gamesmanship more brutal and self-annihilating for companies. But that's another topic, for another day.

As is true throughout *About Face*, my focus here is on the *emotional* factors that influence the creation of effective marketing. So let's stop to consider the psychological, ie emotional, reasons why price-oriented advertising can be problematic for any brand, but especially those that are not intentionally and consistently positioned based on price.

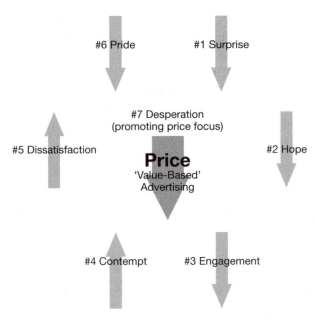

It's not just prices that drop when companies take a 'value'-based advertising approach. Responses to the advertising, the offer or the brand being advertised may also take an emotional hit if consumers get a gnawing sense that the company following this approach has had its confidence shaken, giving a feeling of desperation that hardly encourages loyalty. It's our survival instincts, after all, that cause us not to want to be on a sinking ship.

PROBLEM 1: LACK OF SUSTAINABILITY (SURPRISE FADES)

From an emotional perspective, the first reason why a company's advertising shouldn't lead with price is that discounting – especially if repeatedly relied on – undercuts the key attention-getting advantage of a sale: namely, surprise.

Don't underestimate the value of surprise. It makes our eyes open wide and our jaw draw open. Surprise aids stopping power. We become fully alert, visually taking in the world around us while simultaneously ceasing to talk. In a state of surprise, we wonder whether the cause of surprise will prove to be a threat or an opportunity for pleasure. Surprise is, however, also a very brief emotion. Surprise that lingers on somebody's face for more than a second is almost surely a false expression of shock and awe.

As an emotion, surprise isn't sustainable. And it isn't sustainable as an advertising approach, either. Sooner than later, if a company makes a pricing deal a frequent – or worse, consistent – part of its messaging, then there's no surprise left.

A sale to clear out inventory is understandable. The implication can be that next year's model, for instance, is better than this year's. Moreover, like a President's Day Sale, or a seasonal, quarterly or once-a-year event, it's the exception, not the rule. But a 'sale' that's a daily reality is no longer a surprise; instead, it becomes an expectation.

Advertising (counter)example: What's the opposite of putting the focus on the price, introducing yet another low price that is meant to be today's 'surprise'? It's to let the surprise happen for us based on the unexpected ways the offer proves to be helpful. In China, LG's advertising approach is to sell its phones as a long-term ally. The message is that LG's phones provide ongoing surprises by serving as 'magic weapons' that enable businesspeople to triumph, winning in unusual ways, much like the great ancient Chinese warriors always did.

PROBLEM 2:
BECOME NUMB TO PRICE (DEVALUING HOPE)

A surprise that inevitably fades is no longer a surprise. But from an emotional perspective, that's not all that changes. The longer or more frequently that a company relies on price-leading advertising, the more we expect low prices. With that expectation comes desensitization, robbing a 'sale' price of the wow 'high' that accompanies a pleasant, genuinely unexpected surprise.

Here's scientific proof of what I mean. In a study conducted by Brian Knutson and George Loewenstein, the question was whether showing 'bargain' price tags to shoppers would cause: 1) delight; 2) disgust; and/or 3) the analytical part of their brains to light up most. To learn the answer, fMRI brain scans were done on college-student volunteers as products were shown, followed by price tags at bargain levels.[1]

Fortunately for everyone in business, the first key finding was that seeing most products created some degree of delight. However, seeing *any* price tag caused disgust as well as the start of analysis. Both reactions make sense. Disgust happens because giving up money, a resource, rarely pleases us. Meanwhile, analysis occurs to figure out if the price tag represents a good deal or not.

It's in predicting purchase intent, however, that the study got really interesting.

In that case, the study found that whenever the disgust level exceeded the delight level, the college students *always* chose not to buy the product. In contrast, if a student's delight was greater than the disgust felt, then the verdict swung in favour of making the purchase. As for the analytical part of the brain, it proved to be of no importance in predicting purchase intent.

Purchase decision depends on whether reward outweighs disgust

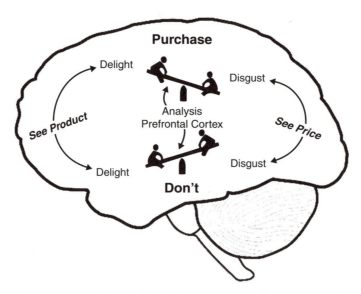

Seeing a product creates delight, but is it strong enough to outweigh the disgust that arises at the thought of surrendering cash to buy it? Unfortunately, disgust levels rise more readily as we acclimatize to a low price. So emphasizing the reward, instead of a low price, becomes the only feasible long-term strategy.

What does this study mean in terms of advertising? It's not only that delight versus disgust is the key equation, so that the role of advertising must be to heighten the offer's allure. It's also that this study found that the 'wow' of a low price wasn't a reliable, sustainable ally in creating allure. Instead, over time the delight-oriented part of the brain acclimatizes to even big bargains, not experiencing as much of a 'high'. As a result, the disgust-oriented part of the brain gains more sway and is then free to nix the potential purchase.

Put another way, the ultimate problem with price-leading advertising is that companies trying price reductions aren't over the long term creating delight or even stoking hopes of delight. Instead, they're merely reducing the disgust, or pain, we feel about spending our money, which is a strategy that fails over time because, again, a constant low-price strategy can't keep disgust from becoming more intense than delight.

> *The prominent price in the ad affects how I see, definitely. When I see the prominent price in the ad, after that I see the ad to analyse the price is fair or not. Usually, I try to enjoy the ad, but not in this situation.*
>
> Sadaaki Takata, Japan

Moreover, research shows that there are other kinds of pain we often care about more. For example, when some people were tested to learn whether 'hassle free' or 'less expensive' mattered more to them, the results came back in favour of 'hassle free' by a 62 per cent to 38 per cent margin.[2] That's probably because enduring inconvenient hassles are a tangible, ongoing kind of pain, and so easier for us to feel strongly about than something abstract like a price tag.

In contrast, premium pricing can feel better for everyone involved. In testing we did for a household-goods company, for instance, the amount of happiness shown by test participants actually rose by 13 per cent compared with a lower proposed price point. Despite the higher cost, the greater positive response was due to the confidence the higher price instilled in people regarding the product's quality and, therefore, its value.

Advertising (counter)example: At this year's Cannes ad festival, one of the really big winners was Tourism Queensland's 'Best job in the world' campaign. Talk about a case of selling hope! The premise was asking people to audition by submitting video clips to explain why they were the best candidate for a caretaker post that provided a good salary and a chance to explore Australia's Hamilton Island in exchange for a six-month stint submitting blogs to talk up the place as a tourist destination. Total cost of the campaign: $1 million. Total estimated value of the press coverage: $70 million, and climbing.[3]

PROBLEM 3: INVITES ANALYSIS
(UNDERCUTTING EMOTIONAL ENGAGEMENT)

In reality, the problem with a marketing strategy that focuses on less pain rather than more hope proves to be even greater than consumers becoming desensitized to price cuts. It's that a focus on price, ie numbers or statistics and, by extension, rational analysis, ends up making us more desensitized, period. 'Sorry, I wasn't thinking' is a well-established phrase. But in truth, 'Sorry, I wasn't feeling' – or in the case of advertising, 'Sorry, I didn't cause you to feel anything' – should be regarded as even more valid grounds for an apology.

Here are the results of another, non-profit, marketing study, so that you can see how focusing on numbers, on prices, doesn't inspire people to open up their purses and wallets.

In this case, Loewenstein teamed up with Deborah Small and Paul Slovic to test two versions of a charity request letter for Save the Children. The first version took the rational 'Sorry, I wasn't thinking' approach. It featured statistics about the problems facing hungry, vulnerable children in Africa. The second letter took the 'Sorry, I wasn't feeling' approach and featured the story of a single person, Rokia, a seven-year-old girl from Mali.[4]

The study's participants were given either the rational/statistics letter or the emotional/story letter, and asked to donate. While those who read the statistics donated on average $1.14, the story version led to people contributing on average $2.38 – over twice as much. There's also an interesting extra twist. A third group was given both the statistics and the story. In response, those who got both letters chose to give only $1.43 on average.

Wow, what was going on here? How could it be that adding statistics actually made people *less* charitable than if they only got the story version of the charity request letter?

Here's the answer, and how it pertains to advertising and the rule of don't lead with price. Quite simply, engaging in analysis reduces our charitable instincts. We don't think our feelings, we feel them. Moreover, thinking gets in the way of feeling. Or as Chip and Dan Heath summarize the researchers' conclusion in *Made to Stick*: 'Once we put on our analytical hat, we react to emotional appeals differently. We hinder our ability to feel,' thereby making marketing much less effective because 'For people to take action, they have to *care*.'[5]

> *When the ad points out my needs or touches my heart, then I would feel like the price is right.*
>
> Chester Chu, Taiwan

Advertising (counter)example: In Argentina, Walmart is urging people to ignore the Great Recession – and not give in to desensitization and gloom. As a result, the tagline has changed to 'No ahorres' ('Don't save') from 'Save money. Live better.' No, it's not that Walmart is abandoning its long-time price-positioning strategy. But it is trying to create a stir, and sales, by advocating the culturally in-tune message of 'Don't hold back your laughter, your kisses, your playfulness. Do not save on learning, on love, on air, on change. Save only money.'

PROBLEM 4:
LOW-VALUE PERCEPTIONS (INVITING CONTEMPT)

So far in enumerating the adverse emotional dynamics of taking a price-oriented approach, my focus has been on the implications for the advertising itself. Now it's time to shift focus to the problems that price-leading advertising creates for the offer being promoted.

Most times, the goal of advertising is or should be to take a customer-centric perspective in making the offer into the hero of the ad. In other words, the advertising should make this clear: the offer's the hero only to the extent that the offer helps the customer *emotionally* and *functionally* at least as much as it financially helps the company making it. But a problem with price-oriented advertising is that it can inadvertently make the offer into the goat, instead.

That's because 'value'-oriented advertising is tricky. Our perceptions are inevitably involved and, in regards to the value = quality/price equation, while price at least gives the illusion of being a precise, tangible entity, visible for all to see, quality perceptions are anything but precise.

Instead, quality is in essence a matter of emotionally based belief. So in the case of new offers, for instance, where quality isn't established yet, the value equation can't really function because one of the two key variables (quality) is an unknown. What will a lower price do? Why, it might help to *shape* perceptions that the as-of-yet floating, undetermined quality of the new offer is actually quite low.

Conversely, if quality is well established (and favourable), advertising a deal might then lower our perceptions of the offer's quality because we begin to wonder – and perhaps believe – that something is wrong. Who hasn't in their own experience hesitated to buy the lowest-priced item in the store because of fears that low price equals low quality? Indeed, to that point research has shown that deep discounts do undermine faith in an offer's value. Research has likewise shown that in the example of distilled spirits, focus groups say that the high-quality brands (the category leaders) are smoother – even though blind-taste panel results indicate no discernible differences.[6]

> *If a product is expensive because it does lots of things or something unique, then it would have to be clearly put across in the ad. Value is the key, rather than price.*
>
> Tony Hodgson, England

Prices are certainly easier to tamper with than quality perceptions that build slowly but can deflate almost overnight. Still doubt my point? Well, here are two additional research examples, with specific numbers, that may or may not convince you (it's all a matter of belief anyway, *right?*)

A product becomes a bonus gift available with the purchase of another product. Does serving as a bonus gift harm that product's value? Yes; in fact people now see it as worth 35 per cent less, on average, than they would have otherwise.[7]

College students pay either full price or at a discount for an energy drink. Then both groups are asked to solve a series of word puzzles. Multiple rounds of testing lead to the identical conclusion: those who paid discount prices solved about 30 per cent fewer puzzles than those who paid full price, leading to the placebo-effect conclusion that since we 'expect cheaper goods to be less effective, they generally are less effective, even if the goods are identical to more expensive products'.[8]

Put another way, cheap doesn't feel good. It's easy to feel contempt for what we perceive as beneath us. We instinctively want what's best in life. A bargain-hunting savvy shopper can feel like they are the best – at being a smart shopper. In that scenario, the bargain is also the best. But the product itself rarely gets seen that way, putting extra pressure on the advertising campaign to establish that the offer's (reduced) value (still) exceeds its cost.

Advertising (counter)example: To improve sales, the Dutch Lady company decided to try a new market and new strategy as well. In Vietnam, they introduced the concept of Mother's Day and made tulips synonymous with it. A stroke of genius? Probably, for by tying perceptions of their new offer to something else well known and presumably treasured (dear old mom), value can get established and maintained more readily.

PROBLEM 5: A PRICE FOCUS DISTORTS PURCHASE CHOICES (DISSATISFACTION RESULTS)

Earlier we saw how taking a rational approach desensitizes people (in that case, to donating to a charity). But taking a price-oriented, statistical, hence rational, approach can also ruin our satisfaction by distorting our decision-making process.

Here's how. In trying to give ourselves (or others, as in traditional market research) a reason why we may or may not buy something, we strain to be rational. We strive to provide smart, safe, justifiable answers – and in the process, tend to undercut the sensory–emotive aspects of making a choice that we will truly like. Or as Jonah Lehrer notes in *How We Decide*, 'When the rational brain hijacks the mind…you cut yourself off from the wisdom of your emotions, which are much better at assessing actual preferences. You lose the ability to know what you really want.'[9]

The perils of over-thinking emerge all the time. But here's a trio of specific examples to show why price-oriented advertising isn't doing a company any good if it risks creating dissatisfaction because we don't go with the option that feels best.

In the first case, some college students were asked to rank which jams tasted best based on blind taste tests. These results matched the rankings made by experts from *Consumer Reports*. Then a second group of students were asked to rank the jams they tasted *and* explain their preferences. As a result of having to justify their choices, the match-up between the results for this new group and the experts dropped by over 40 per cent.

In a second case, college students chose posters for their dorm rooms. Half the group had to explain their choice, half didn't. In the end, 75 per cent of those who had to justify their choices regretted them later, whereas that was true of only 9 per cent of the 'non-thinking' group.[10]

Sometimes ads show prices in order to make you feel the price is right, even if the price is not right. I feel the price is right when you feel that you really would pay for that good.

Nina Arends, Uruguay

In a third case, my company identified ads that we've tested that were statistically driven and likely to distort people's decision-making process by giving them numbers to justify their decision. Would the extra thinking required affect their emotional responses to the ads, we wondered. The verdict? Live by the numbers, die by the numbers. But mostly you die. What our review found is that ads where statistics are prominent do more poorly than other ads. The amount of negative feelings went up by 12 per cent on average, including a 5 per cent increase in frustration probably caused by having to think harder.

As with the last problem, the problem here is that price-oriented advertising undermines the offer. Price isn't an inherent need or want of anyone's.

It's an artificially imposed abstraction. In contrast, pleasure and meaningfulness are far better arbitrators of value. A campaign that steers us by price and away from our true instincts about the offer won't enhance long-term satisfaction or customer loyalty.

Instead, price steering enhances the risk of buyer's regret. It's as if advertising guided by price assumes you won't otherwise be happy with the offer, ironically ensuring that you won't be because it's not what you would have bought if the price hadn't tempted you away from your true instincts. That's why in China an ancient proverb is, 'A cheap price is a shortcut to being cheated.'

PROBLEM 6: BRAND LOYALTY AT RISK (PRIDE TAKES A HIT)

Speaking of loyalty, it's time to move the focus again. First, it was on the potentially adverse effects of price-leading advertising on the advertising itself, then on the offer, and now on brand equity. In fact, my final two problems with a price approach to advertising involve brand equity, starting with the issue of customer loyalty.

Clearly, such an approach often gets adopted in hopes of sacrificing short-term profitability in favour of a long-term gain in a company's market share. But while that strategy might look good on paper, emotionally it risks creating a disconnect if loyalty, a long-term feeling, gets decimated, rather than nurtured and sustained.

Unless carefully enacted, there's nothing to differentiate how current loyal customers versus prospects get treated. Both groups get the new, lower price, even though one group, the current users, had enough belief in the branded offer's value = quality/price equation to buy at what had been the established price point. Yes, new users may get induced to trial. But loyal users who are seeing their belief in the quality/price relationship suddenly undermined – instead of rewarded – may now see the brand as opportunistic in pursuing others, or indifferent to them – and in either case, not worthy of respect.

Moreover, the company loses twice over. Its existing customers pay less for goods they were already buying anyway (and may not buy again at full price, when or if it gets restored, because their latest belief is that the original full price suddenly looks too high). As for the new customers who bought a deal, their loyalty is less real than the profit margin sacrificed to bring them into the picture.

Advertising (counter)example: Consider the example of Mini USA, the US division of BMW's Mini Cooper brand. Eager to capitalize on its car owners' intense loyalty and sense of esprit de corps, Mini decided to market through word of mouth by pitching its current *owners* – rather than focus, as advertising usually does, on prospective *buyers*. So Mini USA sent its owners a decoder package as a prelude to launching ads that had coded messages only they could read.[11] In politics, that's called 'energizing the base'. In the new age of advertising, it deserves to be simply called *smart*. Inspiring feelings of pride in your target market protects and enhances yet another feeling: loyalty.

Following the money versus the dream of other new customers

Inside
the Mini
Spy Kit
Sent solely to owners,
it's a playful way to
generate buzz
around the brand

SUPER-SECRET DECODER

"SECRET" BOOK Although it may blend in on a shelf, the covert kit is more cutesy than crafty. The cardboard book won't fool anyone.

DA MINI CODE Magazine readers see jumbled text. With the decoder, a Mini owner can make out the address of a site that contains special offers.

MAGIC WINDOW The edges on the plastic window bend and block light, arranging snowy fuzz on the roof of a Mini pictured in an ad into a message.

I SPY SWAG Those nose-tinted shades may look dorky, but Mini bets owners will don them if it means getting free car accessories.

Here's a novel approach to advertising that should be imitated more often. Rather than expensively pursue new customers, how often do companies appreciate and reinforce their ties with existing customers: the real money trail? Rarely, unless you count the totally dull letter of appreciation that might come with the latest billing notice, for example. In this case, the Mini Cooper folks don't just dare to have a unique car; they've created a fresh way of reconnecting with current customers, too.

PROBLEM 7:
BRAND INTEGRITY AT RISK (DESPERATION DETECTED)

The final, remaining emotional problem with price-oriented advertising is, again, related to brand equity. It's that using such an approach – repeatedly – means that a brand so often 'on sale' is a brand with an integrity problem. After all, a key way we judge the trustworthiness of others, as well as companies, is to look at the degree to which they behave consistently.

As a result, a company whose advertising occasionally leads with price, like during a recession, is likely to have problems with its integrity three times over:

● First, the company's identity becomes fuzzy. As Denise Shiffman says, 'Your product sells on value or it sells on price. You can't do both.'[12] A company that begins to rely on a price-leading approach in its advertising is signalling that either it is a discount brand or else that it's willing to risk being seen as one. Clearly, some companies aim to position themselves based on price. But for those who don't and yet adopt a price-leading approach to their advertising, a lack of confidence – even desperation – may get inadvertently revealed.

- Second, a company's viability becomes a question mark. Emotions are very contagious. So a company's lack of confidence will also be felt, in kind, by consumers, including most notably current brand loyalists who begin to doubt the company's ability to survive. In short, panic feeds on itself – especially in an era of globalization where competitors are ready, willing and able to knock you off by finding a cheaper way to go to market.
- Third, a company's positioning turns hollow. Leading with price suggests you have nothing else to say, or show, in your advertising. As Gertrude Stein perhaps unfairly said of Oakland, California, 'There's no *there* there.' Price as your main attribute doesn't mean anything – except that instead of emphasizing customer connectivity, aided by advertising, the battle ends up getting fought in terms of price and distribution. Loyalty ceases to be a barrier to entry, as surprise, hope – and every other positive emotional dynamic required – come crashing down.

In summary, the health of your company's value equation depends on your customers having strong emotional ties to your branded offer. A 'deal' secured on price terms puts those buyers *ahead* of the company (they 'won,' securing a great deal), rather than *with* it as a loyal ally who will buy at full price many times again.

Advertising (counter)example: In a nod to Hindu faith, ICICI Prudential has been running a campaign that reassures consumers with the message, 'We live a long time, so no need to worry.' The company even dares add: 'Future guaranteed: no tension'. (In contrast, General Motors' recent announcement of a 'Total Confidence' package for buyers of their cars is, emotionally at least, a complete and utter non-starter: bravado from a seriously wounded warrior.)

IN CONTRAST, THREE REAL SOLUTIONS TO ECONOMIC HARD TIMES AND PRICE/VALUE WARS

None of what I've just written is meant to suggest that facing competition from lower-cost competitors isn't a dire threat to a company, a threat that must be confronted one way or another. It's just that there are better approaches, ones that reinforce the don't lead with price rule. So let me end the chapter with what a company's advertising can do to present real solutions to price competition.

Promote offers with new sensory dimensions to them

The first solution is to go the tangible, sensory route. As mentioned in Chapter 1, advertising should leverage our five senses. Establishing value –

over price – to defend a higher price point can be done by adding offer features that introduce unique tactile sensations, such as a proprietary sound, smell or taste; then leveraging it in the advertising. These kinds of innovations have the advantage of playing to the sensory–emotive connection, rather than relying on more obscure, functional attributes that we may not notice or respond to in an emotional way.

Offer design that introduces sensory appeal value lends itself nicely to the tangible world of advertising. Moreover, to the extent that such innovations occur thanks to customer input via internet feedback channels, companies can later share the news of their responsiveness via those same channels.

For example, Wrigley's new 5 gum claims to 'stimulate your senses' – all five of them. And in the process, it's stimulated revenue growth as well. The company lifted its net sales by 15 per cent over the previous year, using the 5 gum as the primary source of new income. What makes it work? Wrigley's ability to promote it as an all-encompassing sensory experience helps to differentiate the offer. So does a textured package, using black, instead of the usual vibrant colours associated with confections in order to make it stand out in the marketplace.[13]

Enhance brand associations

A second approach is go for greater, more emotionally powerful and unique brand associations. This approach is vital because 'What your brand stands for in the mind of the consumer is as important as – or in many cases more important than – what you make or do.'[14] To capitalize on that reality, in Japan Nestlé's Kit Kat snack benefits from the lucky coincidence that, in Japanese, *kitto katso* means 'surely win'.

Therefore, Nestlé's agency, JWT, thought of partnering with Japan's Post Office to create Kit Kat Mail. These postcard-like versions of Kit Kat were then made available at the country's 20,000 postal outlets, where people could buy and send them immediately to students as an edible good-luck charm just prior to exams. As a result, Nestlé hopes to create a new tradition (sending Kit Kat snacks to students) as well as instil the symbolism of Kit Kat snacks as a good-luck charm.

> *I always try to make sure the brand is coming through. I still believe that you can support the brand while driving price. Give them a reason to like your company and maybe they'll give that company some credit for having a personality, or at least treating the customer as if she has a brain.*
>
> Scott Mackey, creative director, Mackey, Inc.

Beyond brand offer associations, another aspect of uniqueness extends to brand characters, spokespeople, icons and the like. Indeed, Ipsos has found that 'The more a brand has extra appealing emotional associations, the greater the purchase commitment to the brand,' and that ads with a brand character in them test well above norm.[15]

In Allstate Insurance's case, the company has used the calm, assured and reassuring Dennis Haysbert as its on-camera spokesperson for half a decade now. What's new is that for its 'Back to basics' campaign, Allstate put him against a gallery backdrop of Dorothea Lange's black-and-white photographs from the Great Depression to open a script in which Haysbert acknowledges the current hard times, but says that Allstate, founded in 1931, has weathered 12 recessions and is happily still there for its customers.

Rather than fight on price, Allstate has a new website application that offers money-saving tips and promotions – for *other* companies' offers, such as restaurants or Sam's Club. As a Leo Burnett account director has been quoted as saying, 'the category dynamics are all 'price, price, switch and save,' but Allstate isn't going there.[16]

Use innovation and co-creation

If there's a third option, well, it's more general. It's to try new ways to connect, period, given that nowadays the situation is fluid and requires adaptation. A case in point is in the much-hammered real-estate market, where Realogy Corporation, the parent company of Century 21, Coldwell Banker, and Better Homes and Gardens Real Estate, among other brands, has recognized that its communications strategy must change because consumer behaviour is changing.[17]

To that end, newspaper advertising is being replaced by innovations such as informal blogs from company executives, online video tours of homes, and Coldwell Banker's branded YouTube channel.

Will it all work well? Probably not, but the point here is that as we demand more transparency regarding the offer itself, including price, the smart way to play the game will be to promote openness, sharing and collaboration on behalf of making a company's value = quality/price an equation we can buy into. Speed and interactivity will be vital, co-creation inevitable. Only then can companies be assured that we will honour the value put forward in advertising because we will have, in fact, had a hand in designing the offer.

SUMMARY

Companies would like to think the scenario goes like this: We have the same quality as before, but with a lower price. So we're a greater value.' Not exactly. Closer to reality is that as the price dips, many of us perceive the quality as declining, too, leaving the value equation just where it was before the whole deal-oriented advertising campaign kicked off. The one difference? The company is now making less money from customers it already had.

Have I made it clear that I'm not a fan of anything more than the judicious, occasional use of discount pricing? I suspect so. But so as not to leave it in doubt, let me quote Kevin Joy, VP of BrandProtect, regarding his point that 'value' has become 'the most overused and least believed statement in branding'.[18] And that's not a good place to be.

Takeaways include:

- In tough economic times, it's tempting for companies to resort to value-based promotional advertising. In doing so, however, they neither alleviate the brutal price-comparison battle that the internet helps to spur, nor necessarily avoid inviting contempt from consumers who may then see the offer as cheap.
- A price-leading ad approach can prove to be harmful because it robs the marketing of emotional hooks such as surprise, hope, engagement, pride and satisfaction. Not only is the advertising adversely affected, however, so too is brand equity. A desperate company conveys desperation, which consumers will flee from rather than embrace.
- Instead, three better approaches to price competition are: improving the offer's sensory attributes; enhancing brand associations; and demonstrating innovation, often by inviting consumers into the process based on the co-creation of new ideas.

9

Mirror the
target market's values

ORIENTATION

Inevitably, how we view the world and a company's advertising gets 'bent' through the prism of the values we hold. Values reflect beliefs, which are the essence of selfhood. So no company should be at odds with its target market's values. Otherwise, the company and its advertising can't create the kind of enduring emotional connection that translates into market share, because brand loyalty requires honouring the values of the people you're selling to.

Pride is the operative emotion here because we believe in what we believe; it encapsulates our upbringing, influences and life experiences. There's no backing down, no other place to go. As a result, our values can't be changed by companies or their advertising agencies. Nor can they be ignored, because especially among today's younger, social media crowd, yesterday's consumers have become creators and critics, too, putting their own spin on advertising based on what they believe to be important and real.

WHY EMPATHY HAS BECOME
MARKETING'S NEW TOUCHSTONE

Smart companies know that communication isn't only about technology (tools and tactics), but also about winning hearts and minds, which is an emotional consideration. In today's world, addressing the values people have internalized is essential, and depends on gaining an appreciation of other cultures. Why? Consider the following information.

By 2050, the list of the world's 17 largest economies will look very different from today's.[1] The G7 nations (the United States, Japan, Germany, the UK, France, Italy and Canada) will collectively see their economies shrink by 22 per cent on average. In striking contrast, those of the so-called BRIC block (Brazil, Russia, India and China) will experience an average rise of 489 per cent. Turkey and Indonesia will have also become more prominent, surpassing Germany and the UK, and will both approach Japan's new status as the world's fifth largest economy. In rank order, the largest economies of the world will be China, the United States, India and Brazil.

Distribution of global headquarters in 2000

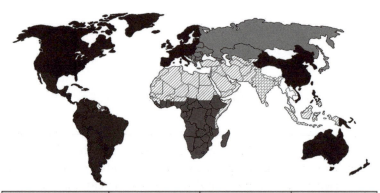

Civilization	Population	Difference	2000 HQ's
■ Western	15%	45%	60%
■ Orthodox	5%	(3%)	2%
▨ Islamic	18%	(16%)	2%
■ African	7%	(6%)	1%
■ Latin American	10%	(7%)	3%
■ Sinic	25%	(13%)	12%
▦ Hindu	17%	(14%)	3%
□ Buddhist	1%	(1%)	0%
▦ Japanese	2%	16%	18%

Today, only the Western world (the United States, Canada and Europe in particular) as well as Japan host more major companies than they do their share of the world's population. But by 2050, the West will most likely constitute only about 11 per cent of the world's population, while Japan's population is also ageing fast. As markets shift away from their home base, companies will either fade or arrest or avoid that fate by becoming more empathetic to cultures vastly different from where their headquarters are located.

Today the headquarters of the largest 2,000 companies in the world are disproportionately based in the West or Japan: 78 per cent of them, to be precise. In business, where getting beyond a company-centric perspective is difficult, note that in 2050 the West and Japan will together most likely constitute barely over one-tenth of the world's population. Then think about the changes and challenges ahead.

In physical terms, the reigning centres of economic power are utterly divorced from what the world now looks like, and where it is increasingly headed toward. As a result, new major companies will of course be arising in China and India, and elsewhere. Meanwhile, today's big companies must face the possibility that they are not only physically but also may become *emotionally* separated from emerging and future markets, and will need to adapt to remain relevant.

That's demographically driven change.

More subtle, more intimate but no less significant are all the changes that are happening *internally* with regards to consumers' expectations of how companies will relate to us. Those changes have occurred with growing force as the internet eclipses TV as both the dominant communications medium and a mindset for how to interact with others. Let me explain more fully, first by showing this model, then by explaining each of these four shifts in consumers' expectations.

The new advertising model

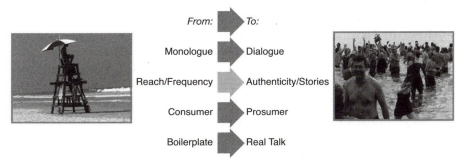

In a word, interactivity has become the key to fostering empathy. Companies must begin to truly understand their customers better. That's because in many cases companies will no longer be selling to us; people who are proactive creators and critics (on the internet) are going to be able to control the medium, the message and even the casting involved. (Before this chapter is over, I'll be talking about resistance or blowback to traditional corporate advertising, and more.)

Here are these four shifts, and what each one means:

- Monologue to dialogue. The era of advertising that we're now leaving behind has been called the Age of Interruption. Through unidirectional shouting and repetition, companies tried to make themselves heard by using TV (and, to a lesser extent, radio, print, etc) as bullhorns to talk at consumers. In the new era, treating the internet as merely a spam-generating bullhorn won't work, however. Consumers now increasingly want and expect dialogue instead. Blogs are one way to accomplish this goal; Twitter and other social media can fit the bill as well.
- Reach/frequency to authenticity/stories. Again, the mass-media broadcast model of advertising was about one (the company) to many (a mass-market audience). But as the marketplace has splintered (cable TV stations, etc), reach and frequency are in doubt and the influence has shifted over to what consumers will accept more readily: advertising that feels more authentic and real, in part by telling stories that people instead of products star in.
- Consumer to prosumer. A company's target market is no longer, actually, a receiving target at all. They're brand loyalists instead, people who increasingly expect (and by the way, deserve) to be treated as a company's partner, invited to join both one-to-one and one-to-many dialogues. As for the term 'prosumer', it dates back to 1980, when the futurist Alvin Toffler published *The Third Wave*. In it, Toffler predicted that some day (now) the world would be increasingly populated by people who don't want to be consumers any longer; they want to be prosumers: pro-active consumers who want to exert influence over the creation of products – and advertising too.[2]
- Boilerplate to real talk. Nobody wants to dialogue with somebody talking corporate speak. It's not authentic, and there aren't any (interesting) stories. So forget about the usual boilerplate language in which companies proclaim product features. As anybody who's ever been in a serious relationship knows, real talk involves praise and criticism, and not just echoing the old broadcast shouting that used to dominate the airwaves. In a democratized marketplace, brand values – wanting to know what a company stands for – outweigh product features that quickly become me-too commodities.

THE STRUGGLE TO CREATE AUTHENTIC DIALOGUES: WELCOME TO EXECUTIVE BLOGGING

By 2006 the observation, 'Every company is a media company,' had begun to be commonplace. Its appearance was a sign of the shift now upon us, as companies must learn how best to communicate in today's internet/social media era.[3] The Realogy Corporation innovations that I gave examples of at the end of the previous chapter, eg executive blogs and Caldwell Banker's YouTube channel, are truly signs of the time.

Given the changes required in everything from style to content and channels, executive blogs are one way to evolve the marketing/communications effort in response to people's preference for more uncensored content and open conversations. While not necessarily the best or exclusive vehicle for dialogue and relationship building, they represent a means of creating an ongoing connection between a company and its audiences.

Now you might ask 'Why bother?' Is trying to create a respectful 'dialogue' (or at least a candid monologue) really a worthwhile use of an executive's busy time? Moreover, what's so bad about giving a monologue that reveals a mass-media mentality? To answer at least the last question, I had my staff check how consumers emotionally respond to TV/radio spots when they feature dialogue instead of a voice-over monologue.

Here's what we found regarding that question, and whether style (more personal versus more formal and professional sounding) might also make a difference in our emotional response.

Monologues are monotonous and too frequently used

From the results, it's clear that talking in a stiff, impersonal style doesn't suit people. Not only is it boring, but that approach doesn't give people a sense of the person talking, a heartfelt voice, a set of values, somebody to relate to. Learning that led me to wonder, in turn, how easily executives will find it to steer their companies toward a communications style that involves not just dialogues but also real talk and authenticity. How easily can they get past sounding like a stuffed shirt?

To find out, I first went in search of guidelines for executive blogging. I couldn't find many, though in an article titled 'Writing the Codes on Blogs',[4] I came across this quote from Sam Phillips of Sun: 'A blog is the authentic voice of the author.'

Reading that comment made me think of 'Boogergate' and how the president of Domino's Pizza handled that crisis. I'm referring of course to when the company was caught in a social-media firestorm because a pair of renegade employees filmed themselves defiling a soon-to-be-delivered sandwich, leading to approximately 1.5 million viewings online. The company president responded with a video of his own, but did he say the right things? Was he appropriately on-message?

Yes, *but* the guy also sounded and looked wooden, tired and sad, and was glancing off-camera as he read his script. In a word, he was *off-emotion*.

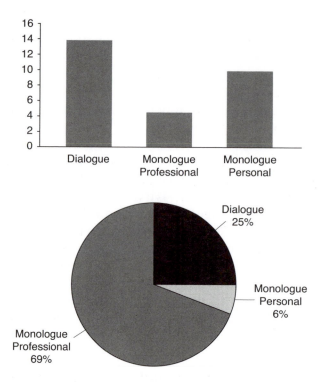

Is dialogue more emotionally appealing? Absolutely. In fact, from our review we found that a dialogue is three times more appealing than hearing a monologue. Meanwhile, adopting a more intimate personal tone is twice as appealing as a colder, more professional approach. So it's too bad that in advertising the least appealing route, a professional-sounding monologue, also happens to be the one chosen most often (69 per cent)!

Moreover, that script was full of corporate-speak, most notably when he referred to the two offenders as 'team members'.[5] *What* team is that? Give Domino's Pizza half a point for real talk.

Would executives fare better in the blogosphere than in a video message like the one Domino's Pizza posted on the internet? With so many choices to consider, I happily came across a blog posted in July 2006 by Mario Sundar, billed as the 'community evangelist and chief blogger at LinkedIn', with his list of the top 10 CEO blogs (all techies, listed in no particular order of ranking).[6] Looking them over, I decided to focus on seven and critique them using seven qualities for the new era of marketing.

Leader	Average	Authenticity	Respect	Empathy	Collabo-ration	Humility	Fun/Interesting	Meaningful
Craig Newmark, CEO Craigslist	6.6	7	7	7	7	7	7	4
Mark Cuban, CEO Dallas Mavericks	5.0	7	5	3	3	3	7	7
Alan Meckler, CEO Jupiter Media	4.6	7	4	4	3	5	5	4
Matt Blumberg, CEO Return Path	4.4	5	3	7	4	5	3	4
Jonathan Schwarz, CEO Sun Microsystems	3.7	4	4	2	2	3	4	7
John Dragoon, CEO Novell	2.4	2	3	2	3	2	2	3
Kevin Lynch, Chief Software Architect Adobe	2.3	2	2	2	2	2	2	4
Average	4.1	4.9	4.0	3.9	3.4	3.9	4.3	4.7

A couple of really good bloggers. Otherwise: just a notch above mediocrity pretty much describes what's on display here. Would these leaders accept that level of performance in their subordinates? Doubtful. If you're going to write a blog, make it inviting.

As you can see, even this group of supposedly excellent bloggers wasn't always that great. My conclusion is that if their CEOs are any indication, most companies' marketing styles will be hard-pressed when it comes to creating brand personalities and interactive approaches that display empathy and authenticity instead of sounding like another press release. No wonder one person posted this comment to Sundar's blog: 'I think it's the very special cases who will take on the risks and challenges of talking *with* their customers and not *at* them.'

THE BATTLE OF SEXISM: OFFENSIVE GENDER PORTRAYALS

It's not just the gap between executives and the average consumer that leaves in doubt the ability of companies to meaningfully interact with their target markets and reflect their values. If there is another, even bigger, gap, surely it's the one that separates the sexes, as represented by the typically male CEO as well as CMO (chief marketing officer) and the typically female shopper, who is the source of much of the company's revenue.

Consider the case of Dell Computer's Della, for instance. Upon launch, that female-targeted microsite quickly got panned in *Advertising Age* for multiple sins,[7] including:

- a clichéd, even hackneyed colour scheme of soft, unthreatening pastels.
- a since-removed image of three colour-coordinated women sitting side by side, so close in fact that their shoulders overlapped – shoulders swathed in fabric that matched their laptops.
- non-technical 'Tech Tips' related to using computers to help count your calorie intake as well as search for recipes online.

Now, that might be an altogether too-funny-for-words attempt to 'spare women from having to confront the full-strength Dell site' if it wasn't also so revealing. Companies still struggle not to offend the values of people – women, in particular – regarding how we get marketed to, even in the 21st century. As *AdAge*'s columnist Teressa Iezzi conclusively adds, 'Historically, marketers have done a less-than-stellar job at recognizing females as both human beings and as important consumers of their products.'

> *The perception is that it's okay for a man to age, but not a woman. This should change in advertising. Sexism says that sex and how a woman looks are the most important thing, instead of using her talents and her brains, and that is so offensive to me.*
>
> Kersti Oja Kringlie, United States

Old and new paths

Three points need to be made here. The first is that nobody in business should doubt the financial importance of the female shopper as a reason for why showing respect is in order. Consider the statistics in the United States, which are likely to reflect reality in many other countries, too. In the United States:[8]

- Women are estimated to be responsible for 83 per cent of all consumer purchases, including: 80 per cent of healthcare decisions, 91 per cent of general household purchases, 94 per cent of furnishing purchases, 92 per cent of vacation expenditures, and 62 per cent of car purchases.
- Today, over 30 per cent of women earn more than their husbands.
- Women also control over 50 per cent of the private wealth (a number certain to rise given their longer life expectancy.)

So shouldn't it set off alarm bells inside company headquarters to learn that 91 per cent of women believe that advertisers don't understand them and 58 per cent are seriously annoyed by portrayals of their gender? (By the way, the numbers aren't much better for men – with 79 per cent of men feeling alienated, barely able to recognize themselves in the ads portraying their gender.[9])

Second, to return to my theme of empathy: isn't it true that we tend to relate best to people more or less like ourselves? In that case, across the realm from companies to their advertising agencies, how well do the typical CMO and typical creative director do in terms of reflecting both the demographic profile – and the values – of the female shoppers so vital to the marketplace?

Let's start with the CMOs at the 25 companies in the United States that spend the largest amount of money on advertising, versus the average shopper. What do we find?

In regards to all but being middle aged and white, it's a big mismatch. The average consumer is female (52 per cent) versus the 80 per cent of CMOs who are male. Meanwhile, the average consumer isn't located in one of the country's 25 largest cities (only 11.5 per cent) and has a household income of $63,000. In contrast, the typical big-company CMO will live in a major city (70 per cent) and earns about $1.5 million.

If it weren't so hard to find a source for their collective profile, a similar divide (almost Grand Canyon in scale) could no doubt be put together regarding chief creative directors at the major ad agencies and the average consumer their ads are directed at. My informal checking into the matter led me to conclude that the vast majority of creative directors continue to be men, even though the number of female creative directors is on the rise.

> *So much of advertising is run by young people, you know, young funky men, and they are marketing to women. And just because you have a kid doesn't mean you are not a person or a woman. You had a life before kids, you had a job. There is more to them than nappies and air fresheners and grocery shopping. Don't underestimate your audience; engage with them.*
>
> Carrie Longton, co-founder, Mumsnet Ltd

Third, none of this is to say that the powers of imagination and empathy can't help cross the gender divide. But it's a large, fundamental divide, and it requires real talent and sensitivity to consistently leap across it without being patronizing, dismissive or simply downright oblivious in little subtle ways and big ways alike. Companies and their agencies may like to think that nothing's wrong. They may think that they're duly sensitive to – and mirror and honour – the target market's values.

But consider the considerable evidence to the contrary:

● Accounts gone awry. At Burger King, TV spots like 'SpongeBob Square-Butt', in which attractive young women engage in dance steps that show off derrieres padded into squares, have caused pushback from women's groups who feel demeaned, as well as from fretting franchise owners.[10] From female Miller Beer employees suing the company for its use of scantily clad, busty models to Motrin moms feeling like they're being patronized (by the brand of painkiller of that name; see below), we've been here before.

● Having critiqued countless TV spots over the years, who's better qualified than *AdAge*'s Bob Garfield to conclude that 'so much advertising sex is neither charming nor artful nor remotely to the point', providing 'tight close-ups of the fully endowed as a gift of fantasy for the not yet fully evolved'.[11]

● Checking on the combined emotional responses of both genders to ways in which they are depicted in both TV and radio spots that we've tested, my company has found that the way mothers get stereotypically portrayed results in the least amount of emotional engagement (only 27 per cent) and the second lowest level of emotional appeal (behind female 'sexpots').

What's the solution? If traditional market research can't catch these failures to respect and mirror the values of both genders early enough in the concept-to-production process of ads, then a new approach is required. Maybe it's time to utilize internet panels of consumers or social-media feedback to gain input before the budget's been spent and the egos are invested in a campaign, to ensure ads that will build on beliefs and attitudes the target market has already internalized and accepted.

THE RISE OF A CREATIVE CLASS
OUTSIDE THE ADVERTISING AGENCY STRUCTURE

When the Motrin moms backlash came, the form it took was revealing. Yes, there was one woman who posted a video of her statement on YouTube, deploring the TV spot in which aspirin is being sold to young mothers to relieve the stress of carrying a baby in a sling. 'Disrespectful', she says, adding that in trying to 'relate to us' the spot is 'actually patronizing us'.

But a parody commercial of the Motrin spot soon also broke on YouTube – substituting breast implants for a baby, and saying the burden of carrying such a heavy load isn't on behalf of the baby but, rather, the husband. At the time of writing, it's drawn 82,681 hits online compared with 276,663 for the original spot.

As if you probably didn't already know this, welcome to the emerging class of creators who don't occupy a cubicle or office in an advertising agency somewhere in the world. The numbers are staggering. As documented in *Groundswell* by authors Charlene Li and Josh Bernoff, the creators who publish blogs or their own web pages, upload newly created videos, music, etc, and/or write articles and stories and post them, represent nearly 20 per cent of adults in the United States, 10 per cent of the online populace in Europe, and percentages of 30 per cent or more in parts of Asia.[12]

The craziest thing about these numbers, however, is that the estimates are just for adults. What about kids, especially rebellion-prone teenagers? In 2005, the Pew Internet & American Life Project released its findings. Its conclusion? More US teenagers are creating content for the internet than are simply consuming it.

What does it all signal? Even if companies – as evidenced by everything from lame executive blogs to sexist, demeaning ads – don't realize, accept and practise the new advertising model shown earlier in the chapter, they'll be forced into authentic, real-talk dialogue full of stories anyway. In short, it's the prosumer wave that Alvin Toffler predicted almost 30 years ago.

In the following section, I'll discuss online critics. But for now my focus is on the creators, a group that should open wide the eyes of CMOs and ad agency executives alike. Put simply, creators are coming soon – and often – to a town near you to remix, and perhaps even bury alive, your advertising executions and, at times, challenge entire brand strategies.

Forget about changing the values of these creators. That isn't going to happen. Instead, let me provide this update. In *Emotionomics*, I wrote that companies should figure out what values emotionally matter most to their target markets and deliver on them.[13] Writing three years ago, I urged companies to be forever on the move, proactively understanding us as our maturing values and lifestyles shift. My advice: mirror our preferences by speaking to us on our level: who we are and associate with, what we do and value.

All of that still holds true, except that given the trend lines of online participation, now the creators must be factored into every advertising campaign – even when they're not part of the target market. One way to understand why is to look at some statistics from YouTube.

Company/Product	Original Ad Hits (+)	Parody Version Ad Hits (-)	Hit Gap
Apple Mac vs PC	1,201,585	13,075,264	−11,873,679
Dove's 'Evolution'	9,116,665	2,105,014	+7,011,651
Snuggie	11,786	5,118,424	−5,106,638
MacBook Air	165,987	3,017,167	−2,851,180
World of Warcraft	2,400,000	762,627	+1,637,373
Olive Garden	54,813	1,083,177	−1,028,364
Dove's 'Onslaught'(er)	97,910	878,751	−780,841

Clearly, on a volume basis the parodies do very well in terms of attracting viewers. In five cases out of seven top-drawing cases where a parody is in play, the parody outdraws the original TV spot – by an average margin of 4,328,140 viewings.

Nor is the volume gap alone the full story here. The Snuggie parody, The 'WTF blanket' – ie the 'What the f*** blanket' – spot, is mostly just entertaining in its withering mockery of the product's value. Truth be told, the Snuggie blanket looks goofy. So in making us wonder about using the product, it's by no means as potentially upsetting to a wide audience of current or potential users as, say, the Coca-Cola/ Mentos mini-mockumentary, which has drawn over 1.5 million hits by showing what happens to Mentos mints if dropped into a glass of Coke (they explode).

Still another level higher up in threatening a company's sales, however, could be the Dove 'Onslaught(er)' parody. This spot has been carefully altered by the environmental activist group Greenpeace, using high production values to make its point. And the point is that the seemingly very ethical stance taken by Unilever – to use real-life models in their ads as a step in protecting the self-esteem of young girls from a beauty industry that will harm them with impossibly high standards – is invalidated by Unilever's allegedly creating products that in the process destroy the beauty of Indonesia's lowland forests.

As a result of this parody, Unilever is taking the need to work with the dynamics of social media seriously. Indeed, the 'Onslaught(er)' parody put all companies on notice. As a result, no company can now release advertising – especially a TV spot – without considering how it might be co-opted (artistically) or create a backlash (politically). More broadly, no brand is immune. Companies prefer to think of their brands as something they control. No longer.

In reality, that was always true: 'Your brand is whatever your customers say it is.'[14] But it's even more true today, and in the future the reality is that it's not just that marketing monologues must become dialogues. It's that the dialogues will increasingly not consist of brand advertising at all – except as a jumping-off point. That's because prosumers will be conversing among themselves on the internet, using everything from newly created and doctored videos to blogs, forums, ratings and reviews to do so.

Companies won't be able to control the outcome. They can only hope to influence how the conversation proceeds. To improve their odds of liking what happens, however, companies can keep in mind – and act on – the qualities I introduced earlier in critiquing the executive blogs. In other words, to be successful in the new era of creators, marketers must join the 'conversation' in a way that will elicit a warmer emotional response, and a better opportunity to reflect and connect on a values basis.

CAUSE MARKETING: A WAY TO NEUTRALIZE CRITICS AND MAKE NEW FRIENDS

First, I should define what I mean by critics. The term refers to people who post ratings and reviews of products or services, contribute to online forums, comment on other people's blogs, and/or may contribute writings to a wiki, for instance. People in the creator or critic category can overlap. In the United States, critics represent 25 per cent of the adult population. The percentage stands at 20 per cent in Europe and 30 per cent in Asia, while climbing all the way up to 46 per cent in Hong Kong.[15]

At the positive end of the spectrum, 96 per cent of the sites that offer a ratings and reviews feature consider them effective in helping to lift the buy rate. For instance, Procter & Gamble's beinggirl.com website (on behalf of selling Tampax and Always) gets over 2 million visitors a month worldwide. When negative attitudes and feelings get unleashed online, however, the best a company can do is to try to re-channel the criticism and learn from it.

For instance, an angry 'Dell sucks. Dell lies' blog posting, with the warning 'we are in the new era of "Seller beware"' was one of many such monologues that ultimately inspired Dell to create an online dialogue with customers. As a result, initiatives such as a cross-departmental 'blog resolution' team and IdeaStorm got launched, to connect more transparently and quickly, as well as tap into the ideas customers might have regarding either solving another customer's problem or generating future design improvements.[16]

Spinning straw into gold is never easy. Type in 'sucks' after just about any company's name and you could be on the internet for hours, maybe years, reading stories of unhappy customer experiences. And I do mean stories. Time after time, phrases like 'Here's the story' – followed by references to hours or even days spent *waiting* for help, or resolution, or redress – appear on the internet. A Russian novel couldn't be bleaker.

Truth be told, the angry stories are, by a factor of at least five to one, longer, more passionate and engaging than most of the positive entries on companies' official websites. But there's hope. I say so based on the uplifting personal stories submitted by us when a company supports a cause we care about and helps make a difference. It's no surprise, then, that in the United States, for example, cause marketing has grown from around $100 million in 1990 to over $1.5 billion by 2009. Success breeds success. Nor for most of us is the Great Recession an acceptable reason for companies to curtail that growth in spending. Indeed, a survey found that 78 per cent of us expect companies to maintain or increase their support of non-profit causes despite the current economic downturn.[17]

Mainstream and alternative examples of cause-related marketing

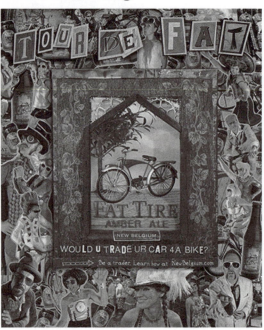

On the left side is copy from Jiffy Lube's website, talking about the parallel universes of taking care of your car's body as well as your own (guarding against heart disease). Is it a stretch to make the comparison? Perhaps slightly, but the cause is good. On the right side is copy from the website of the New Belgium Beer company. It's signature initiative? Well, there's more than one. But easily the funniest and the most fun is sponsoring in multiple cities, a Tour de Fat take-off on the Tour de France bike race. As it turns out, bicycle enthusiasts and the New Belgium Beer's target market overlap nicely, leading to the company's 10 Commandments of the Tour de Fat, including: Put no means of transport before thy bike; May every generation come forth; and, of course: Thou shalt not steal thy neighbour's bike.

Remember that in Chapter 7, the deepest, most profound cause of happiness is when we enjoy a sense of meaning in our lives. That cause is why cause marketing works. It helps bring us together for a purpose greater than ourselves, and when a company can be seen in that light, then the company and its target market are meeting on a values-mirroring basis.

Moreover, in terms of generating goodwill and fostering brand equity, it's a gift that keeps giving. That's because as a rule of thumb, we long to be consistent. We want to stay true to ourselves. It makes us feel more grounded, well oriented and secure. A sense of belonging to a brand, as yours, can feel good. So it's no wonder that Robert Cialdini suggests that one way to achieve influence and persuasion is to 'Focus your messages on how purchasing and using the product are consistent with the audience's pre-existing values, beliefs, and practices.'[18]

SUMMARY

Burger King's 'Whopper sacrifice' campaign – in which consumers were awarded a free Whopper in exchange for de-friending 10 people on Facebook – was a clever way of going against the general ethos of the new online social-media phenomenon. Before the campaign ended because of privacy concerns, a quarter of a million 'friendships' were sacrificed for some free food, sacrificing in the process social affinity for sensory-satisfying expediency.

But in general, look at sites from YouTube ('Broadcast yourself') to Facebook ('Connect and share with the people in your life'), Twitter ('A service for friends, family'), MySpace ('Be a part of the MySpace community'), Flickr ('Share your photos'), etc. Sharing, friendships and a sense of community are the operative concepts. And underlying the whole phenomenon is an instinct for values-based cooperation, collaboration and fairness that reflects the inequality aversion bias I introduced in Chapter 7 as one of the key principles of behavioural economics. That's because, despite Burger King's anti-social foray, most times the internet sensibility rewards respect while punishing what seems unfair or phony and is, therefore, ripe for parody or other forms of criticism.

New media bring new mindsets, emphasizing a point made in one of the executive blogs I critiqued: 'What will the internet squash next?'

Takeaways include:

- The optimal strategy is always to sell consumers on themselves. Advertising should mirror the values, beliefs and attitudes of the target market as much as possible. That's because values reflect beliefs, which are the essence of selfhood.
- Due in large part to the influence of the internet, the new advertising model involves a shift from monologue to dialogue, from reach and frequency to authenticity and stories as important criteria, from consumers to proactive 'prosumers', and from boilerplate language to real talk.
- Sensory Logic's results have found that a dialogue is emotionally three times as appealing as a monologue and that an intimate personal tone is twice as appealing as a colder, more professional approach.

- When it comes to blogging, executives are fairly good at being authentic and providing meaning. However, they struggle with empathy, humility and especially communicating a collaborative spirit.
- Yesterday's consumers have become creators and critics, too, putting their own spin on advertising. As a result, the risk of parodies or other forms of blowback should become a point of consideration in every campaign strategy.
- Gaps in income level and location augment the basic gender gap between the typical CMO and creative director and their often largely female audience. Gender insensitivity continues to be a major factor that blunts the effectiveness of advertising.

10

Believability sticks

ORIENTATION

Yes, trust is the emotion of business. And being an emotion, trust is in essence a gut check that in this case weighs the potential gain of buying the offer against both the certain loss of cash (the offer's price) and uncertainty about whether or not the promised gain, the advertised gain, will in reality prove to be true. In other words, this final chapter of *About Face* is about persuasion and purchase intent, ie our internal, emotional battle between trust and reassurance versus scepticism about being over-promised.

While many factors enter into persuasion, the code word for making money, it's tempting to give clients a definite answer to the question 'Will this ad help me sell more?' But in reality it's not as simple as that because of factors like brand equity, price and distribution. Nevertheless, armed with facial-coding results I'll provide a sense of what ads appear to sell better – and why – using as my organizing principle three types of ads: argument, endorsement and narrative.

THE BATTLE BETWEEN
BELIEF AND PERVASIVE SCEPTICISM

Assertions of trustworthiness are everywhere in advertising. A Reynolds Wrap ad promises, 'Trust every delicious morsel to Reynolds.' A Duracell ad says, 'Trusted everywhere'. Not to be outdone, the computer consulting firm EDS states, 'Trust is not given, it's earned, and EDS earns that trust a million times a day.'

Careful handling: hitting all the right notes

Advertising that can credibly claim that your precious belongings will be carefully treated can help to build market share, being persuasive by building trust.

The good news for companies is that we have an innate desire to trust, to find an ally, to believe in benevolent goodwill. How else to account for the fact that simply asserting trustworthiness – one time, in a single line of text – could lift research scores dramatically? The test in question involved a fictitious automobile service firm called TriStar Auto Care. Sixty undergraduates rated their degree of faith in TriStar, based on ads that did or didn't end with the statement, 'You can trust us to do the job for you.'[1]

Amazingly, adding this simple line lifted trust/confidence ratings by 20 per cent on average.

What simply asserting your trustworthiness can do for a company

However, there's also plenty of bad news when it comes to the issue of trust and advertising. In another study, a combination of undergraduate and graduate business students were asked to imagine themselves in the shoes of a fictitious character named Dave. Then test participants had four different scenarios described to them, involving two variables (the taste of the pizza advertised, and the amount of advertising exposure prior to eating it):

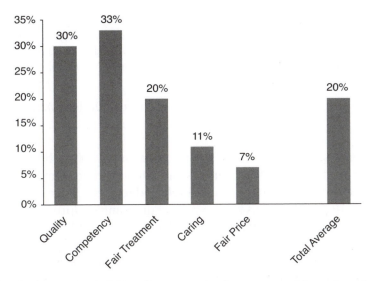

What kind of company is TriStar? By asserting its trustworthiness in a single line of copy, the company saw its quality and competency score climb by 30 per cent or more: further proof that trust is, indeed, the emotion of business.

- 1st scenario. The pizza is advertised only once, as tasty; and when it is eaten, the pizza proves to be tasty.
- 2nd scenario. The pizza is advertised only once, as tasty; but in fact tastes lousy.
- 3rd scenario. Prior to eating the pizza, test participants are exposed to advertising about the pizza three times. The pizza is advertised as tasty; and in fact is tasty.
- 4th scenario. Prior to eating the pizza, test participants are exposed to advertising about the pizza three times. The pizza is advertised as tasty; but in fact tastes lousy.

So what were the results of this test? Scepticism rules. In scenario three, where the pizza was as good as the advertising promised but the test participants were exposed three times to advertising for the pizza, they became nearly as sceptical as participants were in scenario four (when the pizza actually tasted bad). The conclusion? Scepticism serves as a coping mechanism, a way of pushing back, in reaction to a barrage of advertising – no matter how honest the advertising proves to be. Only good pizza rarely advertised (scenario one) helped to lower disbelief.[2]

> *I think advertising has to respect women and our intelligence. Don't tell us an air freshener is going to transform our lives. I don't have a problem with advertising, but I want to find out about things via advertising in an honest way.*
>
> Carrie Longton, co-founder, Mumsnet Ltd

Should that single test result worry advertisers? Yes, because other consumer feedback, such as surveys, has documented similar problems with scepticism. Earlier in this book, I referred to one US survey that found that under 10 per cent of us say we believe in (company/product) information that we learn from advertising. Welcome to a credibility gap that has reached crisis proportions.[3]

Meanwhile, overseas advertising does no better. In a global survey, the A C Nielsen company found word of mouth, not advertising, to be by far the most believable source of information about products or services. At the same time, however, Nielsen also found variances in levels of trust of ads by region and country.[4] The survey involved 47 countries, with each country's trust levels aggregated here by continent.

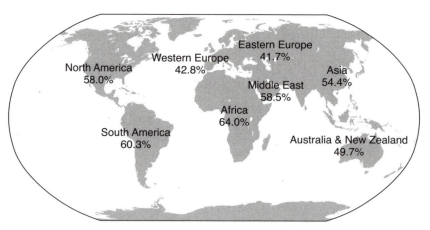

Across all of the regions shown here, our average trust level in advertising is only 53.6 per cent. Put another way, only half of us regard advertising as truthful.

So the sceptical pizza-eating students were hardly an anomaly. Doubt runs rampant. At the same time, the A C Nielsen survey found that trust levels also vary widely according to marketing medium. If newspaper and magazine ads are combined to form the print category, and everything from brand websites to search engine and online banner ads are grouped in the internet category, then here's a five-category comparison:

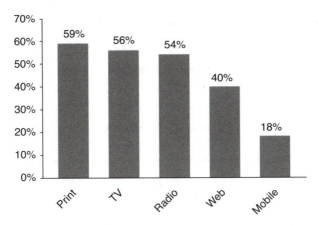

Want your ad to be believed? Then print's your best bet, with TV and radio spots close behind. What's least trusted? For now, the answer is getting advertised to on your mobile device.

In summary, trust is a scarce commodity. Even your supposedly best combination here – using print, in Africa – would only get you into the 60 per cent range. Clearly, the goal of creating persuasive advertising presents a big challenge, but let's not give up. There's more to be said on the topic.

DEFINING THE TYPES OF ADVERTISING

Erik du Plessis of Millward Brown has argued that 'Advertisements that work are advertisements that are liked.'[5] Is likeability the key? It's important, yes. But common sense would suggest that it's hardly determinant of an ad's success in the marketplace. I might enjoy watching a funny TV spot, for instance. But does that mean I'm now going to rush off to buy the offer being advertised?

In a moment, I'd like to use facial coding to help answer that and similar questions regarding what type of advertising is most persuasive. But to do so I must, first, define what types of advertising we're talking about. Aided by a pair of studies,[6] I've created my own framework of three types of ads, each seeking to be persuasive in different ways. One is the argument type, where the underlying goal is to provide *knowledge*. The second type is testimonials, providing *confidence*, given the people who testify on behalf of a company's offer. Then there's the third type, narrative or storytelling, with ads that foster a sense of *affinity* between the situations depicted in the ads and the lives of the target market.

That's by way of overview. Of the three types, argument is easily the most complex. That's because the argument type divides into four subtypes of ads:

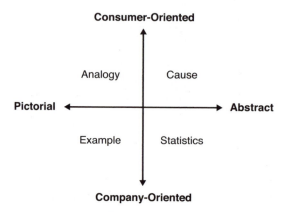

The argument type of ad varies. The analogy and example subtypes are more creatively oriented, as well as more sensory–emotive, relying on visuals to help make their points. That takes care of the pictorial/abstract axis. The other axis here is whether to argue based more on the offer's attributes (company-oriented statistical ads) or based on what the (emotional) benefits are for buyers of the offer (consumer-oriented cause ads).

Examples will probably best clarify what I mean here. From the top right quadrant, around the horn, here's an ad that fits each subtype:

- A cause ad would be something like the batch of direct mailers we tested for Duke Power, arguing for smart energy usage because of the environmental benefits for us all. In other words, 'X causes Y.'
- An example ad would be something like the Canon direct-mail pieces we tested because of their this-feature-equals-this-benefit approach.
- A statistics ad would be something like the famous example of dental health ads stating that '9 out of 10 dentists approve!'
- An analogy ad would be something like the print ad we tested for Astra-Zeneca, touting the solution's simplicity by showing, in contrast, the image of a hedge maze.

In my framework, endorsement ads have no subtypes. But narrative ads have two subtypes, the meanings of which should be fairly obvious from their names. There are humour ads as well as drama ads, with the latter including both problem–solution scenarios and slice-of-life depictions.

WHAT TYPE OF ADVERTISING
IS MOST EMOTIONALLY PERSUASIVE?

Okay. So how do ads of each (sub)type do in terms of persuasion?

To find out, my staff have looked through our database to assemble both emotional and rational results related to purchase intent. The emotional results come from facial coding and are based on the percentage of test subjects whose emotional response was predominantly positive in response to being asked about likelihood of purchase intent, as triggered by exposure to a given ad. As for the rational results, they're based on the percentage of study participants whose comments were predominantly positive regarding likely purchase intent, again in response to the advertising they were shown.

Here's what we found, with the results ranked from high to low based on the degree of emotional buy-in per (sub)type of ad:

Purchase Intent			
(Sub)Type	Emotional (Facial Coding)	Difference	Rational (Verbal Input)
Arguments – Analogy	61%	3%	64%
Arguments – Cause	53%	17%	70%
Narratives – Humour	46%	18%	64%
Arguments – Example	43%	19%	62%
Testimonials	42%	31%	73%
Narratives – Drama	39%	4%	43%
Arguments – Statistics	35%	33%	68%

The two sets of results (emotional and rational) produce very different rank orders. For instance, the statistics subtype comes in third rationally but in last place based on facial coding. The average results are also very different. Across all seven (sub)types of ads, the emotional results average 45.6 per cent buy-in versus 54.2 per cent for the rational results: evidence yet again, I believe, of people saying 'yes' when they really mean 'maybe' or even simply 'no'.

Overall, what's most noteworthy here? For starters, it's that three of the four argument subtypes of ads do really well, coming in first (analogy), second (cause) and fourth (example). Only the most hard-core, rationally oriented argument approach – statistics – fares poorly, coming in last. Meanwhile, the narrative and testimonial types run almost neck and neck because, among narrative's two subtypes, humour does relatively well (third place), while drama comes in sixth.

Before I move on to analyse the results, there's one other set of comparisons that will aid in the conclusions I draw. It involves how well each (sub)type of ad does on its first exposure (initial view) versus how we respond to it later, after at least one subsequent viewing, when purchase intent is at stake.

Why should you care to know? The answer is because the results can help to either verify or refute Erik du Plessis's belief that a liked ad is, therefore, a successful ad. How we feel initially, after all, when not much more than our gut reaction is involved, may not reflect how we'll feel when the idea of giving up money for the company's offer is now at stake instead. Here are the results as they progress from first exposure to subsequent, purchase-intent exposure based on using facial coding alone to identify the percentage of test subjects whose emotional response is predominantly positive:

Does intial reaction predict likely purchase intent? Not exactly.

(Sub)Type	Initial View Emotional (Facial Coding)	Difference	Purchase Intent Emotional (Facial Coding)
Arguments – Example	51%	(8%)	43%
Arguments – Analogy	51%	10%	61%
Arguments – Cause	50%	3%	53%
Narratives – Drama	50%	(11%)	39%
Narratives – Humour	48%	(2%)	46%
Testimonials	43%	(1%)	42%
Arguments – Statistics	39%	(4%)	35%

Two (sub)types of ads improve their performance in the move from initial view to a test's concluding purchase-intent stage (when an ad is being experienced for the final time). Those that do better over time and when money's at stake are the analogy and cause ads. Statistics remain in last place both times. Meanwhile, both example and drama fare less well at the purchase-intent stage.

Again, what's most noteworthy here? In emotional terms, the first-exposure average is 47.4 per cent versus 45.6 per cent during the purchase-intent stage. So in that sense, the results remain remarkably stable across the two rounds of exposure. There is one big gainer and there are two big losers, however, with analogy climbing over 10 per cent in terms of the amount of positive feelings it generates when money's at stake, whereas example and drama both falter badly on subsequent, purchase-intent exposure.

To understand why, and how come all the results may have turned out the way they did, it's time now for some analysis of the results, knowing that du Plessis's conclusion – that (initial) likeability is the key – hasn't proved to be a very reliable barometer of whether the ad will help you make more money or not.

TIME FOR ANALYSIS: WHAT ARE THE IMPLICATIONS OF THESE VARIOUS RESULTS?

Now let's take a closer look at each of the three types of ads, including subtypes when they exist. My purpose here is to understand why each (sub) type fared as it did, and what kind of insights and guidelines advertisers might take away from it all. Here is what I believe, mixing data with instincts honed by over a decade of experience conducting emotionally oriented research projects.

Argument

The underlying rationale for using this approach is that there presumably exists *objective* evidence that the offer represents a smart, defensible, superior choice. How can the objective evidence be introduced? This type covers four choices, which in emotional terms performed in descending order of effectiveness as follows: analogy, cause, example and, finally, statistics. The question is, why?

Analogies win because the ads can reach you twice over. There's the message, the argument, but there's also the imagery that's allowed to play a major role in reinforcing the message. Remember how in Chapter 1, on simplicity, I cited a study that found that almost all of the award-winning ads fitted one of six templates? Of them, pictorial analogies were the lion's share at almost 35 per cent. Well, here's proof that analogies not only win advertising awards, they lift sales.

Cause-based argument ads come in second best because the chain-reaction logic of 'X causes Y' is easy to follow. Cause ads give consumers very concrete and, again, *simple* reasons why the offer will prove to be a benefit to them.

To be specific, was the artwork sophisticated for the Duke Energy direct mailers we tested? No. For example, the environmentally friendly statement 'Be good to your mother' was accompanied by (what else?) a photograph of earth shot from outer space. But as Bob Garfield notes in *And Now a Few Words From Me*, a review of the 25 ad campaigns anointed as best ever by *Advertising Age* brought him to the conclusion that 19 of them broke no rules and involved no great creative licence; but they broke sales records.[7] Moreover, cause ads are a close cousin to the consequences template used by nearly 20 per cent of all the award-winning ads in the study cited in Chapter 1.

By comparison, example-based argument ads go from specifics to a general inference (or more rarely, vice versa). Why does this type of features/ attributes approach perform no better than average in regards to purchase intent (but tied for best during the first view)? Maybe it's because when a company talks directly about its own product, at first we feel comforted by getting the picture. But then we find it rather self-serving and boring.

Finally, it isn't surprising that the statistics type of argument ad comes in last emotionally (while in third place, rationally). After all, statistics are quite often dull, abstract and complicated. And, as noted in Chapter 8, numbers can numb us. Moreover, statistics are in trouble when it comes to trust, the key emotion necessary for persuasion. After everything from Enron to the latest financial meltdown, who really trusts how numbers can get spun?

In summary, simplicity, tangibility ('seeing is believing') and presenting arguments from a consumer's point of view rather than using a company's own terms (and numbers) work best here. We want to know what's in it for us, not the company. As a result, the more the argument gets presented in terms where the company's self-interest becomes evident, the harder it is for us to reach the point of an emotionally oriented licence to *believe*.

Testimonials

As already discussed in Chapter 4, celebrity endorsements and the appearances of CEOs, experts or average Jane/Joe Doe consumers testifying on behalf of an advertised offer are all meant to be persuasive, too. In the first three cases, the goal is to draw on the influence of authority figures. As for Jane or Joe Doe, they're meant to provide the social proof that your 'neighbour' finds the offer worthwhile, and so should you.

> *Expert opinion always feels insincere. If the average person can deliver the message in an authentic, humorous way, I generally like the advert.*
>
> Sacha du Plessis, South Africa

Of relevance here is research indicating that if your goal is to boost attitudes toward an offer among people strongly interested in it, famous endorsers are of only marginal help.[8] In short, paying for celebrities to appear in ads may not be worth the expense. Results show famous endorsers to be as effective as 'strong arguments' among low-involvement prospects, but of less help than non-famous endorsers when high-involvement prospects are focused on.

Indeed, neither type of endorser, famous or not famous, turns out to be as helpful as all but the statistics version of an argument ad. Indeed, our results found testimonials to be subpar (whereas the rational results put it in first place). Why? It is doubts about authenticity, an inability to believe, that threatens endorser effectiveness in these cynical times.

Narrative

Any concerns about the effectiveness of more rationally oriented, argument ads are inversely related to reasons why emotionally oriented narratives might have promise. As described by careful advertising analysts ranging from John Philip Jones to Gerard Tellis, among others, the comparison looks something like this, if told from the perspective of why emotional ads should work well:

First, they're more likely to grab attention (rather than require it, like example or statistics ads do). They operate in a subconscious or peripheral way, thereby being better able to cut through the media clutter and engage low-involvement prospects.

Second, they're likely to be more vivid and memorable than drier, rationally oriented ads.

Third, they don't invite resistance from us as we evaluate the merits of an argument and draw our own, potentially different conclusions.

Finally, and perhaps most decisive of all, they leverage the emotional brain's biological importance and do so twice over. For starters, evaluation requires emotions to kick in, intuitively weighing the alternatives. Otherwise, there's analysis paralysis. Moreover, as mentioned earlier in this book, only the older sensory and emotive brains link to the body's muscles, making an emotionally triggered call to action literally more actionable.[9]

No wonder then that in *Effective Advertising: Understanding When, How, and Why Advertising Works*, Gerard Tellis concludes that 'emotional appeals are probably the most effective'.[10] Not only are there the advantages already cited, but Tellis's research also leads him to believe that emotionally oriented ads tend to wear out more slowly and are more likely to benefit from increased media exposure.

In principle and by instinct, I agree with Tellis. Narrative ads of either the humour or drama type should do fairly well. So why not here, in this case, based on our results? Why is humour fifth in initial-view responses and merely third for purchase intent? And why is drama tied for third in initial view and sixth in purchase intent?

The plausible answer lies in the executions of the ads themselves.

In regard to humour, it's something of a high-wire act. Sometimes the humour works wonders. Sometimes it doesn't work at all. Still other times it works but doesn't translate well in regards to its relevancy to the offer for sale (potentially overshadowing it or, worse, undermining it).

For instance, some supposedly funny print ads we tested for a furniture maker involved sexual innuendos. The advertising agency's all-male senior creative team thought the ads made for a good laugh. But in reality they made some of our female test participants so uneasy that words like 'sexual harassment' and 'rape' were said, with profoundly negative feelings also appearing on the women's faces to underscore the emotional depth of their aversion.

As for drama, the casting is as important as the plot. An off-emotion, bad acting job will undermine the outcome as badly as an off-colour joke will undermine a humour ad. Emotionally dull acting ruins the effect. Think of the telecommunications example I described in Chapter 2. You know: the 60-second radio spot with the huge bald spot where emotional engagement disappears once the generic voice-over enters the picture.

THE TWO ENDS OF THE SPECTRUM FOR CREATING PERSUASION

When all's said and done, there are two basic pathways to persuasion. There's argument and there's emotion. Testimonials fall in between rationally oriented arguments and emotionally oriented narratives, while drawing on both ends of the spectrum. As described and verified through independent testing,[11] the criteria for argument versus emotion provide a framework for judging success.

A successful argument ad must create belief without inviting counterargument. As for narratives, they must create engagement and provide authenticity in order to create affinity and win us over. That's it in essence. Here's a full checklist of the goals that each separate end of the spectrum must follow to be persuasive:

Argument/Rational Ads	Narratives/Emotional Ads
Bolster Belief	**Bolster Belief**

FAMILIARITY	FAMILIARITY
– Familiar is true	– Familiar feeds comfort
– Ads need to fit both offer category & brand expectations	– Ads need to enable relating to people & situation

Bolster Belief & Dispel Objections	**Build Empathy & Avoid Fakery**

FAIRNESS	DESIRE
– Ads show respect, sense of reciprocity, and humility; give reason to believe new claims or uniqueness	– Ads leverage core motivations, involve aspirations, hope, passion, purpose, personality
– Practice simplicity, specificity	– May involve sensory pleasure, interactivity
– Show pain/gain contrast	– Utilize suspense
– Avoid giving sense of company as predator	– Avoid being outside social norms, or blurry, hard to follow

Dispel Objections	**Avoid Fakery**

CONSISTENCY	CONSISTENCY
– Offer value is consistent, assure via repetition	– Remain in character, on-emotion, true to plot/situation and target market values
– Use personal pronouns	– Non-verbals must be handled well
– Avoid gyrating strategy, confusion, lack of transparency	– Avoid gyrating tonality, plot, being impersonal

What does it take to succeed? In essence, rational ads aim for us to objectively weigh the evidence and yield to it. We evaluate the information provided, and if we resist it's because we conclude the company is misbehaving in how it has selected the information being provided. In other words, we're getting spun. Meanwhile, in essence, emotional ads aim for us to subjectively process their content and get engaged. We're empathetically involved, and if we resist it's because we sense the actors are misbehaving as part of a script we dismiss as contrived or off-taste. In other words, we either get offended or become dubious.

There could never be a single definitive answer to the question, 'What does it take to create believable, persuasive advertising?' But by drawing on a few sources as well as my own professional judgment of what works, and why, here's some context to explain the chart I've just given you.

FAMILIARITY: WHAT WE KNOW AND LIKE, WE TRUST

First up is familiarity. The rule in Chapter 3, keep it close to home, is a good place to start. Remember what I said then: we assume that what's familiar is true.[12] There's a lot to be said for making us feel comfortable, which familiarity aids. In a study about persuasion, one of the conclusions was that 'commercials that jolt the viewer by their unexpectedness' belong to the lowest category of advertising effectiveness, ie persuasion. In contrast, ads that were seen as fitting expectations about the offer's category were high in persuasiveness.[13]

> *If it's a good company and I have tried one of their products or hear a friend or family member talking about a good experience they had with a product, I trust. Secondly, I generally trust companies that have social responsibility as part of their strategy. BP has endorsed and sponsored so many initiatives and are pioneers of cleaner fuel, which buys my trust.*
>
> Themba Ndlovu, South Africa

Advertising (counter)application: Contrary to leveraging familiarity, General Motors put out a print ad apologizing for previous quality lapses in their motor vehicles. As our facial-coding results showed, brand loyalists took the news hard because it told them that what they thought was familiar and true ('I've been making good choices by buying GM products') wasn't necessarily true at all.

FAIRNESS VERSUS DESIRE: FULFILLING ON PRACTICAL NEEDS OR WANTS AND DREAMS

Second, let's look at fairness versus desire. Fairness pertains to argument ads because we always wonder whether the company selling to us is truly an ally or merely a predator. Is it being honest and upfront, or manipulative, about the information it's giving us? Meanwhile, desire is an important element in narrative ads because they work best if we're drawn into the action in a way that we find meaningful because our personal goals and the value of the offer get linked. In other words, relevancy is confirmed based on desiring and believing that happiness – not merely utility – is what the offer will deliver.

FAIRNESS: WHY HUMILITY AND SPECIFICITY WORK WONDERS

A natural part of buying is, again, to make sure you feel like you're gaining an ally. Put another way, is the company caring, reciprocal and respectful? Robert Cialdini suggests that a little corporate humility (admit your short-comings) can do wonders to reinforce a sense of honesty.[14] That's because arguing against your own self-interest suggests you're interested in a win–win outcome.

For example, Progressive Insurance's advertising showcases its willingness to make the rates of competitors accessible to us by visiting its website. That's far better than the flip side of humility: condescending ads that trigger reactions of disgust and spur rejection.

> *The actual product makes me trust it, not the ad. It has to do with the company as well. I think Aveda and Origins are great because they bring back to the earth and I like what they stand for. They do not advertise a lot, don't over-expose themselves, and you trust the company.*
>
> Jennifer Jenkins, United States

Tactical considerations: While simplicity means there's less to object to, specificity adds the virtue of making it easier to be believable. As Claude Hopkins says in *Scientific Advertising*: 'A man who makes a specific claim is either telling the truth or a lie.' As a result, 'No generality has any weight whatsoever.'[15] What might work even better? Specifics showing a pain–gain contrast because the original, sensory brain is a pattern-matching machine that readily absorbs contrasts.

Moreover, as hackneyed as it may seem, the use of rhymes like 'Gillette – the best a man can get' aren't just easy to memorize and repeat. The ease with which they flow makes them feel right and lifts the perceived trustfulness of the messaging.[16]

DESIRE: IT'S ALL ABOUT THE THREE PS OF PASSION, PLEASURE AND PURPOSE

Let me touch again here on the three Ps described in the Introduction. Narrative ads must create an immediate, intuitive emotional response; that's passion. Next, they will work best if they reflect the target market's values, providing a sense of purpose. Third, they will also work best if both the actors in the ads and the company's brand are presented in a way that has some real character or personality, thereby engaging us.

In support of that goal, advertising that's both sensory in nature and interactive in style can heighten the three Ps. So is it any surprise that one of the new frontiers in advertising involves video games? About 60 per cent of online Americans play the games, often obsessively, so gamers are a highly sought-after market.

Advertising applications: In Unilever's case, its Suave brand has worked with the online game 'The Price Is Right', sponsoring free play and running promotional ads while the game is loading. Not to be outdone, Progressive has integrated itself into Electronic Arts' game 'Need for Speed: Undercover' by having itself billed as the game's racing-stadium owner, complete with its logo and name plastered on in-game billboards. Look for more to come.[17]

CONSISTENCY: NOBODY'S WON OVER BY FICKLE COMPANIES AND MONO-EMOTION ACTORS

Finally, there's consistency leading to assurance. Since the pattern-matching, sensory brain looks for safety in repetition, we naturally interpret 'inconsistency as possible danger'.[18] How might inconsistency manifest itself? With argument ads, that can happen when a company is forever changing its strategy, forever repositioning itself. As for narrative ads, there the problem arises when the talent is emotionally inauthentic.

> *Any time a company talks about a warranty, you feel safe. It if backs you up, then that helps trust. Information also makes you feel safe and when you know they are there to help. A confident voice in an ad helps with trust, too.*
>
> Hugo Martin Feu, Argentina

Let's tackle the companies first. Want to enhance persuasion potential, instead of destroying it? Don't create a feeling that you're 'pulling a fast one' by changing campaigns and brand positioning so frequently. That approach brings the agency new billings, but it doesn't do much for us in deciding whether a company's a solid, stable ally or a desperate chameleon.

Meanwhile, related to consistency is a tip I gave earlier in *About Face*: using 'you' and 'we' in ads. That tactical tip is relevant here because the use of personal pronouns helps to signal a committed, intimate, one-to-one relationship with us. In doing so, a company provides a sense of solidarity with potential customers by portraying the speaker as a member of the target market to be served by buying the offer.[19]

As for the acting talent, facial expressions can be decisive. Here's proof. In studying the impact of political advertising from the 2000 US presidential race, researchers concluded that the candidate's affect, while shown on screen, was the *only* variable that consistently explained changes in voters' preferences in the battleground states they investigated.[20]

One of the pitfalls of the current version of most casting is that it gets decided based on photographs, ie still images. But somebody who 'looks good' is probably almost by definition a person with a social-smile-type personality. Their ability to act and be on-emotion, exhibiting authentic 'looks' both positive and negative, may be inherently limited. Who suffers? The company that pays the bills because its ads won't be nearly as effective, since everyone on the planet is instinctively on the lookout for phonies – and never wants anything to do with them.

SUMMARY

Market researchers love to test for message comprehension. Yes, that's important. But in the end, it's the emotional verdict of message believability that matters most. Nowadays, advertising faces a serious credibility gap. Pushing harder won't solve it. Only trust can overcome either innate or learned scepticism and lead to persuasion. Reassurance is a feeling, or perhaps more specifically it's the absence of negative feelings that warn us, 'Caveat emptor,' to *beware* of buying. First impressions, peaks and endings matter the most. So it figures that Sensory Logic's persuasion data verify that how we feel during the last five seconds of exposure to TV spots correlates highly to positive emotional purchase-intent levels.

Understanding what we have internally, privately, emotionally endorsed is not yet a core competency in the business world. Too often, the unchallenged assumption at corporate headquarters is, 'Give consumers enough features and reasons to be convinced of utility, and faith will follow.'

Not necessarily. Not when so many other purchase options exist in today's global, internet-linked marketplace. On the other hand, some things don't change. Want to goose purchase intent? Then heed Bill Bernbach's words: 'You've got to say it in such a way that people will feel it in their gut. Because if they don't feel it, nothing will happen.'[21] An on-message focus alone fails to grasp the deeper reality that emotions serve as an inner source of energy, information *and* influence.

Takeaways include:

- Persuasion involves an internal, emotional battle between an innate desire to trust the benefits the company's offer will provide and scepticism about being over-promised. While assertions of trustworthiness lift levels of belief remarkably well, scepticism still remains pervasive.
- Three major types of advertising were reviewed to determine relative ability to be persuasive. Argument ads provide knowledge. Testimonial ads use the people who are testifying as a means of instilling confidence. Finally, narrative ads foster a sense of affinity between the situations depicted and the lives of the people exposed to the ads.
- Of the three types, Sensory Logic found that argument ads are the most persuasive because the less hard-sell approaches of both analogy and cause ads work so well. In contrast, narrative ads do only slightly better than testimonial ads, both of which suffer at times from emotional miscues involving either authenticity or sensitivity.
- Emotional responses on initial exposure to an ad weren't found to be entirely predictive of purchase intent/persuasion. Analogy ads did far better on repeat exposure, whereas example and drama ads did significantly worse.
- As to the keys of being persuasive, simplicity, tangibility, and presenting arguments from a consumer's point of view proved to be most important. Successful rational ads avoid inviting a counterargument. Meanwhile, successful emotional ads get the audience empathetically involved.

Afterword

Because I am so often asked for a checklist or some other means of boiling down what I've learned into a manageable set of advice, I'm going to conclude *About Face* with just such a checklist. It isn't long, seven items, a final takeaway.

1. Be on-emotion (and not just on-message). To hit on the right emotion, at the right time, in the right way, on behalf of the right strategy, is golden. For one thing, it means you can leverage the emotion's storyline, its essential meaning, which everyone can relate to. If your ads can evoke sadness well, for instance, then everybody will understand the power of feeling forlorn, without hope, and then hope for the solution's power to change things. For another, by being on-emotion your ads should have the emotional fuel to set on fire a relevant motivation. Finally, by being on-emotion you protect the advertising, the offer and the brand against being false. Authenticity is crucial, and will give the fire you light the required staying power to go along with emotion's pure stopping power.
2. Be in motion. What do people pay attention to? Novelty. Change. Intensity. In a word, motion. That's because all of us either want change or fear change regarding every single aspect of our lives. Tapping into how people want to resolve, evade or mitigate problems raises the prospect of hope, of arriving at happiness that's terribly fragile – and represents an opportunity to sell again and again. As eye-tracking results I've shared with you show, the eye goes where there's either motion (in video) or implied motion in still imagery. And where the eye goes, brain cells and the heart all follow.
3. Don't create a psycho-killer brand. Faces matter a lot in advertising; sometimes I think they're almost the entire game. That's because the

casting and performance of the talent will drive (or kill) engagement. This takeaway in the checklist encompasses the previous two entries, since *facial-muscle activity is motion, motion that should be on-emotion.* Otherwise, you create advertising (and ultimately a brand) where the emotions are missing, or fake, and the target market disengages. Bad news? Absolutely. Only it's probably worse than that. Remember the brain scan of a psychopath? Psycho-killers have missing or off-emotions. A cold, impassive face equates to a cold heart that brings no love. It creates no opportunity for affinity. It won't sell the brand any better than the corner-of-death placement of your company's logo.

4. Create engaging sensory experiences. Go beyond sight and sound to leverage the other three senses of smell, touch and taste that are just waiting to tantalize your target market. Stage events, add new sensory wrinkles, whatever it takes. Try, try, try something new. Getting us to tune in to our own feelings will generate emotional momentum. The Sex Pistols may not be everybody's cup of tea. But I remember vividly being in Virgin Records in London, with 'Anarchy in the UK' playing on the store's overhead sound system. Everybody stopped thumbing through the records. Everybody was immersed. Everybody heard Johnny Rotten belting out 'nooooo future' in exactly the inverse way that you want us to hear your advertising and sing to ourselves, 'greatttt future'.

5. Achieve elegant simplicity. Clutter is the enemy of greatness. Walt Disney knew to ask the bizarre question, 'What's the weenie?' to his Imagineers, wanting to know what was the dominant visual detail in every setting and situation. Steve Jobs urges elegant simplicity. In the end, it's the same thing. Is there a signature detail? An emotional hook? Can you get there quickly? If it takes more than three seconds to comprehend something, anything (including a joke), it won't have nearly the same emotional voltage as it would if it adhered to Wundt's sweet spot: simple but novel, or complex but familiar. Message-itis. Feature-itis. The deathly opposite of engaging in triage and enshrining the core idea. As Vincent van Gogh said: 'Exaggerate the essential and leave the obvious vague.' Enough said.

6. Use emotion, then close with an intellectual alibi. Promote desirability, but back it up with utility. Remember: people buy emotionally but they justify the purchase to themselves (and others) rationally. So you've got to hit them with the power of emotions and then provide the intellectual alibi. The first punch is emotional, striving to go as deep as you can into the heart of happiness, past physical pleasure, past mental pleasure, right to the meaningful essence of promising a sense of belonging and/or security and order. Get there, and you won't invite resistance. You'll be riding on passion and purpose. Then give them the justification they'll

tell themselves, spouse, family and friends. The quality of the offer will be inherently felt, and believed. But fail to be emotionally generous, fail to adhere to the law of reciprocity (let the company come across as a parasite, not a trustworthy ally in the advertising), and everything's doomed.

7. Stay in the comfort zone. We believe that what is familiar is true. How incredible, and how true. Behavioural economics is in essence about the amazing mental gymnastics we go through to protect our sense of well-being. Damn the facts. They're malleable, unlike our gut reactions. Stick close to the heart, close to people's values, and you're home safe (with them). We'll pay big bucks for advertised offers that bolster our pride and make us say, 'That's my brand.'

Notes

INTRODUCTION

1. Garfield, B (2009) Do you even remember any of the Lion-ized campaigns? Thought not, *Advertising Age*, 29 June.
2. Neff, J (2008) OMD proves the power of engagement, *Advertising Age,* 15 July.
3. Pringle, H and Field, P (2008) *Brand Immortality: How Brands Can Live Long and Prosper*, Kogan Page: London.
4. Elliott, S (2004) A survey of consumer attitudes reveals the depth of the challenge that the agencies face, *New York Times*, 14 April.
5. Ries, A and Ries, L (2004) *The Fall of Advertising and the Rise of PR*, Collins: New York.
6. Canabou, C (2002) Advertising under review, *Fast Company*, 62, April.
7. Hallward, J (2007) *Gimme! The Human Nature of Successful Marketing*, Wiley: New York.
8. Briggs, R and Stuart, G (2006) *What Sticks: Why Most Advertising Fails and How to Guarantee Yours Succeeds*, Kaplan Publishing: Chicago.
9. Jones, J P (2001) *The Ultimate Secrets of Advertising*, Sage Publications: Minneapolis.
10. Sullivan, L (1998) *Hey, Whipple, Squeeze This: A Guide to Creating Great Advertising*, Wiley: New York.
11. Ries, A and Ries, L (2004) *The Fall of Advertising and the Rise of PR*, Collins: New York.
12. Locke, C, Levine, R, Searls, D and Weinberger, D (2001) *The Cluetrain Manifesto: The End of Business as Usual*, Perseus Books: New York.
13. Shiffman, D (2008) *The Age of Engage: Reinventing Marketing for Today's Connected, Collaborative, and Hyperinteractive Culture*, Hunt Street: New York.

CHAPTER 1

1. Ries, A and Reis, L (2002) *The 22 Immutable Laws of Branding: How to Build a Product or Service into a World-Class Brand*, HarperBusiness: New York.
2. Kronholz, J (2007) Talk is cheap in politics, but a deep voice helps, *Wall Street Journal*, 3 November.
3. Renvoisé, P (2007) *Neuromarketing: Understanding the 'Buy Buttons' in Your Customer's Brain*, Thomas Nelson: Nashville.
4. North, A (1997) In-store music affects product choice, *Nature*, **390**, 132.
5. Sultry jeans ad banned by WABC, WCBS-TV (1980) *New York Times*, 20 November.
6. Renvoisé, P (2007) *Neuromarketing: Understanding the 'Buy Buttons' in Your Customer's Brain*, Thomas Nelson: Nashville.
7. Empowering women in the Muslim world (2008). http://www.voanews.com/uspolicy/2008-06-02-voa7.cfm.
8. Wallraff, B (2000) What global language? *The Atlantic Monthly*, November.
9. Sullivan, L (1998) *Hey, Whipple, Squeeze This: A Guide to Creating Great Advertising*, Wiley: New York.
10. Blakeslee, S and Blakeslee, M (2007) *The Body Has a Mind of Its Own: How Body Maps in Your Brain Help You Do (Almost) Everything Better*, Random House: New York.
11. Vicente, M, Chasse, B and Arntz, W (writers; television broadcast) (2004) What the Bleep Do We Know!? In *What the Bleep Do We Know!?* Portland, OR.
12. Lindstrom, M (2008) *Buyology: Truth and Lies About Why We Buy*, Doubleday: New York.
13. Ackerman, D (1991) *A Natural History of the Senses*, Vintage Books: New York.
14. Proudfoot, S (2007) Move over scratch-and-sniff: sample taste strips could be new flavor fave, *CanWest News Service*, 3 January.
15. Soucheray, J (2009) A Cadillac... and a ride into a forever-lost past, *St Paul Pioneer Press*, 7 June.
16. Godin, S (2006) *Small Is the New Big*, Penguin: New York.
17. Goldenberg, J, Mazursky, D and Solomon, S (1999) The fundamental templates of quality ads, *Marketing Science Journal*, **18**, 333–51.

CHAPTER 2

1. Restak, R (2006) *The Naked Brain: How the Emerging Neurosociety is Changing How We Live, Work, and Love*, Harmony: New York.
2. Oatley, K (2006) *Understanding Emotions*, Blackwell: Malden, MA.
3. Bierce, A (1999) *The Devil's Dictionary*, Oxford University Press: New York.
4. Briggs, R and Stuart, G (2006) *What Sticks: Why Most Advertising Fails and How to Guarantee Yours Succeeds*, Kaplan Publishing: Chicago.
5. Gigerenzer, G (2007) *Gut Feelings: The Intelligence of the Unconscious*, Viking Adult: New York.

6. Ogilvy, D (1985) *Ogilvy On Advertising*, Vintage Books: New York.

7. Carter, R (1999) *Mapping the Mind*, University of California: Berkeley, CA.

8. Beaird, J (2007) *The Principles of Beautiful Web Design*, SitePoint.

9. Sullivan, L (1998) *Hey, Whipple, Squeeze This: A Guide to Creating Great Advertising*, Wiley: New York.

10. Pieters, R and Wedel, M (2004) Attention capture and transfer in advertising, *Journal of Marketing*, **68**, 36–50.

11. Outing, S and Ruel, L (n.d.) The best of eyetrack III: what we saw when we looked through their eyes. Retrieved 23 July 2009.

12. Luntz, F (2007) *Words That Work: It's Not What You Say, It's What People Hear*, Hyperion: New York.

13. Jones, J P (2001) *The Ultimate Secrets of Advertising*, Sage Publications: Minneapolis.

14. Peoples, D A (1988) *Presentations plus David Peoples's proven techniques*, Wiley: New York.

15. Jones, J P (2001) *The Ultimate Secrets of Advertising*, Sage Publications: Minneapolis.

16. Heath, C and Heath, D (2007) *Made to Stick: Why Some Ideas Survive and Others Die*, Random House: New York.

17. Lehrer, J (2009) *How We Decide*, Houghton Mifflin Harcourt: Boston.

18. Sullivan, L (1998) *Hey, Whipple, Squeeze This: A Guide to Creating Great Advertising*, Wiley: New York.

19. Suarez, B D (1993) *7 Steps To Freedom II: How To Escape The American Rat Race*, Hanford Press: Canton, Ohio.

CHAPTER 3

1. Sutherland, M and Sylvester, A K (2006) *Advertising and the Mind of the Consumer*, Allen and Unwin: Sydney, Australia.

2. Mullman, J (2009) Land Rover taps Twitter as campaign cornerstone, *Advertising Age*, April.

3. Lehrer, J (2009) *How We Decide*, Houghton Mifflin Harcourt: Boston.

4. Carter, R (1999) *Mapping the Mind*, University of California: Berkley CA.

5. Tegler, E (2009) Ford is counting on army of 100 bloggers to launch new Fiesta, *Advertising Age*, 20 April.

6. Carter, R (1999) *Mapping the Mind*, University of California: Berkeley, CA.

7. Restak, R (2006) *The Naked Brain: How the Emerging Neurosociety is Changing How We Live, Work, and Love*, Harmony: New York.

8. Lance, S and Woll, J (2006) *The Little Blue Book of Advertising: 52 Small Ideas That Can Make a Big Difference*, Portfolio Hardcover: New York.

9. Hallward, J (2007) *Gimme! The Human Nature of Successful Marketing*, Wiley: New York.

10. Hart, L A (1975) *How the Brain Works: A New Understanding of Human Learning, Emotion, and Thinking*, Basic Books, New York.

11. Ries, A and Trout, J (2001) *Positioning: the Battle for Your Mind*, McGraw-Hill: New York.
12. *National Geographic-Roper Public Affairs 2006 Geographic Literacy Study* (2006) National Geographic Education Foundation: Washington, DC.
13. *The Potential Impact of a Western Hemisphere Travel Initiative Passport Requirement on Canada's Tourism Industry* (2005) Canadian Tourism Industry: Vancouver.

CHAPTER 4

1. Restak, R (2006) *The Naked Brain: How the Emerging Neurosociety is Changing How We Live, Work, and Love*, Harmony: New York.
2. Perrett, D (1984) Visual cells in the temporal cortex sensitive to face view and gaze direction, *The Royal Society*, **223**, 293–317.
3. Restak, R (2006) *The Naked Brain: How the Emerging Neurosociety is Changing How We Live, Work, and Love*, Harmony: New York.
4. Blakeslee, S and Blakeslee, M (2008) *The Body Has a Mind of Its Own: How Body Maps in Your Brain Help You Do (Almost) Everything Better*, Random House: New York.
5. Ekman, P (2001) *Telling Lies: Clues to Deceit in the Marketplace, Politics, and Marriage (Vol. 3)*, W W Norton: New York.
6. Grandey, A A, Fisk, G M, Mattila, A S, Jansen, K J and Sideman, L A (1996) Is service with a smile enough? *Organizational Behavior and Human Decision Processes*, 38–55.
7. McNeill, D (1998) *The Face*, Little, Brown: Boston.
8. Reidenbach, R and Pitts, R E (1986) Not all CEOs are created equal as advertising spokespersons, *Journal of Advertising*, **15**(1), 31.
9. Banich, M T (2003) *Cognitive Neuroscience and Neuropsychology (Student Text)*, Houghton Mifflin Company: Boston.
10. Sutherland, M and Sylvester, A K (2006) *Advertising and the Mind of the Consumer*, Allen and Unwin: Sydney, Australia.
11. Hallward, J (2007) *Gimme! The Human Nature of Successful Marketing*, Wiley: New York.
12. Brizendine, L M (2007) *The Female Brain*, Broadway: New York.

CHAPTER 5

1. du Plessis, E (2008) *The Advertised Mind: Groundbreaking Insights into How Our Brains Respond to Advertising*, Kogan Page: London.
2. Carter, R (1999) *Mapping the Mind*, University of California: Berkeley, CA.
3. Witt, G A (1999) *High Impact: How YOU Can Create Advertising that SELLS!* Halstead: Scottsdale, AZ.

4. Heath, C and Heath, D (2007) *Made to Stick: Why Some Ideas Survive and Others Die*, Random House: New York.
5. Heath, R (2004) Ah yes, I remember it well! *Admap*, 37, May.
6. Bolls, P D, Lang, A and Potter, R F (2001) The effects of message valence and listener arousal on attention, memory, and facial muscular responses to radio advertisements, *Journal of Communication Research*, **28**(5), 627–51.
7. Woltman Elpers, J L, Mukherjee, A and Hoyer, W D (2004) Humor in television advertising: a moment-to-moment analysis, *Journal of Consumer Research*, **31**.
8. Young, C (2004) Capturing the flow of emotion in television commercials: a new approach, *Journal of Advertising Research*, **202**.
9. Briggs, R and Stuart, G (2006) *What Sticks: Why Most Advertising Fails and How to Guarantee Yours Succeeds*, Kaplan Publishing: Chicago.
10. Hill, D (2008) *Emotionomics: Leveraging Emotions for Business Success*, Kogan Page: London.
11. du Plessis, E (2008) *The Advertised Mind: Groundbreaking Insights into How Our Brains Respond to Advertising*, Kogan Page: London.

CHAPTER 6

1. Ries, A and Trout, J (2000) *Positioning: The Battle for Your Mind*, McGraw-Hill: New York.
2. Sullivan, L (1998) *Hey, Whipple, Squeeze This: A Guide to Creating Great Advertising*, Wiley: New York.
3. Renvoisé, P (2007) *Neuromarketing: Understanding the 'Buy Buttons' in Your Customer's Brain*, Thomas Nelson: Nashville.
4. Lance, S and Woll, J (2006) *The Little Blue Book of Advertising: 52 Small Ideas That Can Make a Big Difference*, Portfolio Hardcover: New York.
5. Decker, B (2007) *You've Got to Be Believed to Be Heard (updated edition): The Complete Book of Speaking... In Business and in Life!* St Martin's Press, New York.
6. Lawrence, P R and Nohria, N (2002) *Driven: How Human Nature Shapes Our Choices*, Jossey-Bass: San Francisco.
7. Briggs, R and Stuart, G (2006) *What Sticks: Why Most Advertising Fails and How to Guarantee Yours Succeeds*, Kaplan Publishing: Chicago.
8. Witt, G A (1999) *High Impact: How YOU Can Create Advertising that SELLS!* Halstead, Scottsdale, AZ.
9. Brinks: Home Security for Modern-day Damsels in Distress. Retrieved from http://jezebel.com/5120866/brinks-home-security-for-modern-day-damsels-in-distress.
10. Davies, R (n.d.) *The 2006 Basic Necessities Survey in Can Loc District, Ha Tinh Province, Vietnam*.
11. Twitchell, J B (2000) *20 Ads That Shook the World: The Century's Most Ground-breaking Advertising and How it Changed Us All*, Three Rivers, New York.

12. Silverstein, M J, Fiske, N and Butman, J (2008) *Trading Up: Why Consumers Want New Luxury Goods – And How Companies Create Them*, Portfolio Trade, New York.
13. Jensen, R (1999) *The Dream Society*, McGraw-Hill: New York.
14. Plutchik, R (1990) *The Emotions*, University Press of America: New York.
15. Thomaselli, R (2009) Fear factor gets Brink's buzz – and a sales boost, *Advertising Age*, 13 April.
16. Mark, M and Pearson, C (2001) *The Hero and the Outlaw: Building Extraordinary Brands Through the Power of Archetypes*, McGraw-Hill, New York.
17. Hallward, J (2007) *Gimme! The Human Nature of Successful Marketing*, Wiley: New York.

CHAPTER 7

1. Ries, A and Trout, J (2001) *Positioning: The Battle for Your Mind*, McGraw-Hill: New York.
2. Klein, S and Lehmann, S (2006) *The Science of Happiness: How Our Brains Make Us Happy – and What We Can Do to Get Happier*. Marlowe and Company: Emeryville, CA.
3. Lehrer, J (2009) *How We Decide*, Houghton Mifflin Harcourt: Boston.
4. Klein, S and Lehmann, S (2006) *The Science of Happiness: How Our Brains Make Us Happy – and What We Can Do to Get Happier*, Marlowe and Company: Emeryville, CA.
5. Holbrook, M and Batra, R (1987) Assessing the role of emotions as mediators of consumer responses to advertising, *Journal of Consumer Research*, **14**(1), 404–20.
6. Seligman, M (2004) *Authentic Happiness: Using the New Positive Psychology to Realize Your Potential for Lasting Fulfillment*, Free Press: New York.
7. Klein, S and Lehmann, S (2006) *The Science of Happiness: How Our Brains Make Us Happy – and What We Can Do to Get Happier*, Marlowe and Company: Emeryville, CA.
8. Gigerenzer, G (2007) *Gut Feelings: The Intelligence of the Unconscious*, Viking Adult: New York.
9. Diener, E and Suh, E M (2003) *Culture and Subjective Well-Being (Well Being and Quality of Life)*, The MIT Press: New York.
10. *Transparency International: Corruption by Country* (2005) Retrieved 31 July 2009 from http://www.nationmaster.com/graph/gov_cor-government-corruption.
11. Van Hoven, M and Aditham, K (2009) Pepsi steals from Obama and Coke brings back the happiness. In *AgencySpy*. Weblog post retrieved 22 January from http://www.mediabistro.com/agencyspy/brands/pepsi_steals_from_obama_and_coke_brings_back_the_happiness_106592.asp.
12. Collier, J (2009) When cola ads collide, *Atlanta Journal-Constitution*, 22 January.
13. Wilson, T D (2004) *Strangers to Ourselves: Discovering the Adaptive Unconscious*, Belknap: New York.
14. Lehrer, J (2009) *How We Decide*, Houghton Mifflin Harcourt, Boston.

15. Hallward, J (2007) *Gimme! The Human Nature of Successful Marketing*, Wiley: New York.
16. Lance, S and Woll, J (2006) *The Little Blue Book of Advertising: 52 Small Ideas That Can Make a Big Difference*, Portfolio Hardcover: New York.

CHAPTER 8

1. Lehrer, J (2009) *How We Decide*, Houghton Mifflin Harcourt: Boston.
2. Luntz, F (2007) *Words That Work: It's Not What You Say, It's What People Hear*, Hyperion: New York.
3. Hall, E (2009) How the world's advertisers cope with recession, *Advertising Age*, 22 June.
4. Small, D, Loewenstein, G and Slovic, P (2005) *Can Insight Breed Callousness: The Impact of Learning About the Identifiable Victim Effect on Sympathy* (scholarly project). In *Working Paper, University of Pennsylvania*.
5. Heath, C and Heath, D (2007) *Made to Stick: Why Some Ideas Survive and Others Die*, Random House: New York.
6. The Impact of Discounting on Brand Equity (n.d.) In *Killian and Company Advertising*. Retrieved 23 July 2009, from http://www.killianadvertising.com/wp3.html.
7. Goldstein, N, Martin, S and Cialdini, R B (2008) *Yes! 50 Scientifically Proven Ways to Be Persuasive*, Free Press: New York.
8. Lehrer, J (2009) *How We Decide*, Houghton Mifflin Harcourt: Boston.
9. Lehrer, J (2009) *How We Decide*, Houghton Mifflin Harcourt: Boston.
10. Lehrer, J (2009) *How We Decide*, Houghton Mifflin Harcourt: Boston.
11. Li, C and Bernoff, J (2008) *Groundswell: Winning in a World Transformed by Social Technologies*, Harvard Business School Press: New York.
12. Shiffman, D (2008) *The Age of Engage: Reinventing Marketing for Today's Connected, Collaborative, and Hyperinteractive Culture*, Hunt Street, New York.
13. Sensory experience: Wrigley's new 5 gum stimulates the senses, (2008) *Goliath Business News*, 1 May (retrieved 31 July 2009).
14. Lance, S and Woll, J (2006) *The Little Blue Book of Advertising: 52 Small Ideas That Can Make a Big Difference*, Portfolio Hardcover: New York.
15. Hallward, J (2007) *Gimme! The Human Nature of Successful Marketing*, Wiley: New York.
16. O'Leary, N (2009) Allstate speaks to troubled times, *Adweek*, 15 January.
17. Miley, M (2009) Real-estate ads find new home on web in recession, *Advertising Age*, 1 June
18. Bulik, B (2009) How your value message can be heard above the din, *Advertising Age*, 6 April.

CHAPTER 9

1. Hawksworth, J (2006) *The world in 2050*, PricewaterhouseCoopers.
2. Toffler, A (1980) *The Third Wave*, William Morrow and Co: New York.
3. Stein, L (2009) PR must lead way to promised land, *Mediapost.com*, 25 June.
4. Pimentel, B (2005) Writing the codes on blogs, *San Francisco Chronicle*, 13 June.
5. Garfield, B (2009) Domino's apology video isn't going to erase those images, *Advertising Age*, 20 April.
6. Sundar, M (2006) Top 10 CEO blogs. In *Marketing Nirvana*, 9 July. Weblog post retrieved from http://mariosundar.wordpress.com/.
7. Iezzi, T (2009) Dell's Della debacle an example of wrong way to target women, *Advertising Age*, 25 May.
8. Barletta, M (2005) *Marketing to Women: How to Increase Your Share of the World's Largest Market*, Dearborn Trade: Chicago.
9. Secrets of the Male Shopper (2006) *BusinessWeek*, 4 September.
10. Mullman, J and York, E (2009) What Crispin's lauded BK work doesn't do: gain ground on McD's, *Advertising Age*, 22 June.
11. Garfield, B (2004) *And Now a Few Words From Me: Advertising's Leading Critic Lays Down the Law, Once and For All*, McGraw-Hill: New York.
12. Li, C and Bernoff, J (2008) *Groundswell: Winning in a World Transformed by Social Technologies*, Harvard Business School Press: New York.
13. Hill, D (2008) *Emotionomics: Leveraging Emotions for Business Success*, Kogan Page: London.
14. Li, C and Bernoff, J (2008) *Groundswell: Winning in a World Transformed by Social Technologies*, Harvard Business School Press: New York.
15. Li, C and Bernoff, J (2008) *Groundswell: Winning in a World Transformed by Social Technologies*, Harvard Business School Press: New York.
16. Li, C and Bernoff, J (2008) *Groundswell: Winning in a World Transformed by Social Technologies*, Harvard Business School Press: New York.
17. Hessekiel, D (2009) The economy may be cold, but cause marketing is hot, *Advertising Age*, 25 May.
18. Goldstein, N, Martin, S and Cialdini, R B (2008) *Yes! 50 Scientifically Proven Ways to Be Persuasive*, Free Press: New York.

CHAPTER 10

1. Li, F and Miniard, P (2006) On the potential for advertising to facilitate trust in the advertised brand, *Journal of Advertising*, **35**(4), 101–12.
2. Koslow, S (2000) Can the truth hurt? How honest and persuasive advertising can unintentionally lead to increased consumer skepticism, *The Journal of Consumer Affairs*, **34**(2), 245–68.
3. O'Brien, T (2005) Spinning frenzy: PR's bad press, *New York Times*, 13 February.

4. *Truth in Advertising* (2007, October) Retrieved from http://au.nielsen.com/site/ Trustinadvertising.shtml.

5. du Plessis, E (2005) *The Advertised Mind: Ground-Breaking Insights Into How Our Brains Respond to Advertising*, Kogan Page: London.

6. Broda-Bahm, K T (2004) *Argument and Audience: Presenting Debates in Public Settings*, International Debate Education Association: New York.

7. Garfield, B (2004) *And Now a Few Words From Me: Advertising's Leading Critic Lays Down the Law, Once and For All*, McGraw-Hill: New York.

8. Petty, R E, Cacioppo, J T and Schumann, D (1983) Central and peripheral routes to advertising effectiveness, *Journal of Consumer Research*, **10**, 135–46.

9. Carter, R (1999) *Mapping the Mind*, University of California: Berkeley, CA.

10. Tellis, G J (2004) *Effective Advertising: Understanding When, How, and Why Advertising Works*, Sage Publications: Thousand Oaks, CA.

11. Deighton, J, Romer, D and McQueen, J (1989) Using drama to persuade, *The Journal of Consumer Research*, **16**.

12. Restak, R (2006) *The Naked Brain: How the Emerging Neurosociety is Changing How We Live, Work, and Love*, Harmony: New York.

13. Kover, A, Goldberg, S M and James, W L (1995) Creativity vs. effectiveness?: An integrating classification for advertising, *Journal of Advertising Research*, 29–40.

14. Goldstein, N, Martin, S and Cialdini, R B (2008) *Yes! 50 Scientifically Proven Ways to Be Persuasive*, Free Press: New York.

15. Hopkins, C C (2008) *Scientific Advertising*, Waking Lion: West Valley City, Utah.

16. McGlone, M S and Tofighbakhsh, J (2000) Birds of a feather flock conjointly: Rhyme as reason in aphorisms, *Psychological Science*, **11**, 424–28.

17. Chiang, R (2009) Game advertising goes mainstream, *Advertising Age*, 13 July.

18. Renvoisé, P and Morin, C (2007) *Neuromarketing: Understanding the 'Buy Buttons' in Your Customer's Brain*, Thomas Nelson: Nashville.

19. Fuertes-Olivera, P A, Velasco-Sacristán, M, Arribas-Baño, A and Samaniego-Fernández, E (2001) Persuasion and advertising English, *Journal of Pragmatics*, **33**, 1291–1307.

20. Huber, G and Arceneaux, K (2007) Identifying the persuasive effects of presidential advertising, *American Journal of Political Science*, **51**(4), 961–81.

21. Renvoisé, P and Morin, C (2007) *Neuromarketing: Understanding the 'Buy Buttons' in Your Customer's Brain*, Thomas Nelson: Nashville.

Picture credits

INTRODUCTION

Page 3, Paginazero (16 January 2005). *German-Manufactured Typewriter, circa 1930* [Photograph]. In *Wikimedia Commons*. Retrieved from http://commons.wikimedia.org Canuckguy (12 November 2006).

Page 5, Carter, R (1999) *Mapping the Mind*. Berkely, CA: University of California Press.

Page 8, *Blank Map-World-v6* [Photograph]. In *Wikimedia Commons*. Retrieved from http://commons.wikimedia.org

CHAPTER 1

Page 13, *Nothing Comes Between Me and My Calvins*. Photograph found in Flickr.

Page 15, *Prehistoric drawings in the Magura cave*. Photograph found in Public Domain, Bulgaria.

Page 16, *Japanese Road sign (Way narrows.svg* (9 March 2007). Photograph found in Wikimedia Commons-Public Domain.

Page 16, *Japanese Road sign (Rotary).svg* (4 March 2007). Photograph found in Wikimedia Commons-Public Domain.

Page 16, *Japanese Road Sign (Slippery road).svg* (5 March 2007). Photograph found in Wikimedia Commons-Public Domain.

Page 16, *Japanese Road sign (Children).svg* (5 March 2007).

Page 16, Photograph Stop sign light red.svg (April 2007).

Page 18, *Quiksilver, Original Thinking-Ramp*. Permission granted: Saatchi Copenhagen & Quiksilver.

Page 19, *Aquain Nosen.PNG* (1 November 2007). Photograph found in Wikimedia Commons-Public Domain.

Page 19, *Pomoc kod entropija-ispravljanje I fiksiranje ruba kapka flasterom. jpg* (17 January 2009). Photograph found in Wikimedia Commons-Public Domain.

Page 19, SpirellaCorsetry07.gif (21 November 2005). Photograph found in Wikimedia Commons-Public Domain.

Page 19, *Earlobes free attached.jpg.* Photograph found in Wikimedia Commons-Public Domain.

Page 19, *Human Brain sketch with eyes and cerebellum.svg.* (6 May 2009). Photograph found in Wikimedia Commons-Public Domain.

Page 22, *Think Small-VW* (1959). In D D Bernbach (Author). Photograph found in Volkswagen of America, Inc, Virginia, Herndon.

CHAPTER 3

Page 48, *Most Marriages Don't Have This Much Unconditional Love-Cubs Forever*. Permission granted: Nuveen Investments/ Fallon Agency, Minneapolis

Page 50, *DOVE Firming Ad. Permission granted: Unilever U.S.*

CHAPTER 4

Page 56, *Look at Mommy*. Photograph found in Flickr.

Page 58, *Acquedotto di Silvio.svg* (23 June 2009). Photograph found in Wikimedia Commons-Public Domain.

Page 59, *La gioconda.jpg (Mona Lisa/Leonardo de Vinci)*. Photograph found in Wikimedia Commons-Public Domain.

Page 60, *Hemispheres.png.* (3 March 2007). Photograph found in Wikimedia Commons-Public Domain.

Page 60, Disgust.jpg (14 May 2007). Photograph found in Wikimedia Commons-Public Domain.

Page 63, *Brain human coronal section.svg.* (23 December 2006). In P Lynch (Comp.). Photograph found in Wikimedia Commons-Public Domain.

Page 63, *Head ap anatomy.jpg.* (2006, 23 December 2006). Photograph found in Wikimedia Commons-Public Domain.

CHAPTER 5

Page 74, Blamires, M. *Sleep before you drive*. Photograph found in Collective Force (Ads of the World).
Page 78, *Cowboy with cigarette*. Photograph found in Flickr.
Page 80, *Ambulance*. Photograph found in Flickr.
Page 85, *Golden Gate Bridge*. Photograph found in Flickr.
Page 85, *Golden Gate Fog*. Photograph found in Flickr.

CHAPTER 6

Page 88, LinkedIn. Photograph found on www.successories.com
Page 88, *iGod*. Photograph found in Flickr.
Page 97, *Hidden Addiction, Pills*. Client: Bellwood Health Services, Inc; Advertising Agency: DONER Canada; Art Director: Amanda Wood; Copywriter: Ash Tavassoli; Account Manager: Andrew Simon; Photographer: Chris Gordaneer (Westside Studios).
Page 97, *The Bold Look of Kohler 'Plane'*: Permission granted by Kohler Co.

CHAPTER 7

Page 104, *Smiley face on spare cover*. Photograph found in Flickr.
Page 105, Human Brain sketch with eyes and cerebellum.svg (6 May 2009) Photograph found in Wikimedia Commons-Public Domain.
Page 110, Open Roads. Photograph found in Flickr.
Page 110, Europa flyer truck. Photograph found in Wikimedia Commons-Public Domain.

CHAPTER 8

Page 131, *Inside the Mini Cooper Spy Kit*. Photograph found in *Business Week*.

CHAPTER 9

Page 139, *JAXNeptunbeach031*. Photograph found in Flickr.

Page 139, *Swimmers 1*. Photograph found in Flickr.
Page 150, *Tour de Fat – Fat Tire Amber Ale*. Photograph permission by New Belgium Brewing Company.

CHAPTER 10

Page 154, *FedEx Express*: Photograph by Marcus Hausser; Agency: DDB Brazil.

Index

NB: page numbers in *italic* indicate figures or tables

1-800-Flowers *67*
3Ps (passion, purpose, personality) 8,
   167–68
7Up 87

ABC 13
AC Nielsen 156
Admap 79
Adobe *143*
Advertising Age 4, 143, 144, 146, 162
   top 100 advertising campaigns 20
   top media spending categories *96*
advertising effectiveness 6
Age of Engage, The 7
Age of Interruption 4, 140
Allstate 48, *68*, 134
American Association of Advertising
   Agencies 6
American Legacy Foundation 76, 77
Ameritest 83
And Now a Few Words From Me 162
Apple 84
   1984 commercial 6
   and brand loyalty 54
   Mac vs PC campaign *147*
   Macbook Air *147*
   Steve Jobs 30
Applebee's *101*

argument advertising 157, *158*,
   161–62, *165*
Astra-Zeneca 158
AT&T *34*
Atlanta Journal-Constitution, The 112
Aziz, Adnan 20

Ball, Harvey *104*
Bank of America *34*
Barrymore, Drew *68*
Batra, Rajeev 105
Bayne, Katie 112
Beaird, Jason 33, 34
behavioural economics 112–17, *114*
   conformity 115
   impulsivity 116
   inequality aversion 116–17
   loss aversion 113
   overconfidence 116
   probability blinders 115–16
   resistance to change 114–15
believability 153–70
   asserting your trustworthiness 154,
      155
   creating persuasion 164–69
      casting 169
      consistency 168–69
      fairness vs desire 166–68

familiarity   166
and marketing medium   156–57, *157*
and region   156, *156*
types of advertising
  argument advertising   157, *158*,
    161–62, *165*
  emotional buy-in by type   *159*,
    159–60
  narrative advertising   158, 159,
    163–64, *165*
  purchase intent by type   *160*, 161
  testimonials   157–58, 162–63
word of mouth   156
Bellwood   *97*
Belushi, John   114
Bernbach, Bill   62, 169
Bernoff, Josh   146
Better Homes and Gardens Real
  Estate   134
Bierce, Ambrose   30
billboards   32
Bird, Larry   *68*
Blake, William   57
Blink   3
Blumberg, Matt   *143*
BMW   *101*, 110
  Mini Cooper   116, 130–31
Boniva   *68*
brain science   1, 73, 113
  and 'bargain' price tags   123–25, *124*
  emotional brain (limbic system)   4,
    5, 13, 89
  and familiarity   47–48, 51
  fMRI brain scans   29, *60*, 68, *69*,
    101, 124
  and happiness   103, 104, *105*
  and language skills   74
  and narrative ads   163
  and probability   47
  processing of faces   57–61
  rational brain (cortex and
    neo-cortex)   4, 5, 14, 41, 129
  and filtering   46
  and pattern matching   21, 167,
    168
  and sensory processing   *19*

right-left brain specialization   33, 59
sensory brain (brainstem and
  cerebellum)   4, *5*, 13, 89
and smiles   65
brainstem   *see* brain science
brand personality   100–02, *101*
brand recall   83–84
Brandon, Dave   *67*
BrandProtect   135
Briggs, Rex   6, 30, 83, 92, 93
Brink's Home Security   98–99
Bud Light Lime   17
Burger King   22–23, *101*
  'Have It Your Way'   21
  'SpongeBob SquareButt'   145–46
  'Whopper sacrifice'   151
Burke   74, 81
Businessweek   112
buyer's regret   2

Café Crown   24
Calvin Klein   13, *13*, 14
Canon   158
Captain Morgan   116
cause marketing   149–51, *150*
  see also argument advertisements
CBS   13
Century 21   134
cerebellum   *see* brain science
Chaplin, Charlie   65
Chrysler   *67*, *68*
Cialdini, Robert   151, 167
Cicero   62
Clow, Lee   6
Cluetrain Manifest, The   7
CNN   63
Cobain, Kurt   51
Coca-Cola   148
  and Santa Claus   75
  'I'd Like To Teach The World To
    Sing'   10
  'Open Happiness'   112
Coldwell Banker   134, 141
Consumer Reports   129
'corner of death'   35–37, *36*, *37*, 84
corruption, fear of   107, 108–09

cortex   *see* brain science
Costco   *34*
Cover Girl   *68*
craigslist   *143*
Crawford, Cindy   *68*
creative templates
   competition   24
   consequences   23
   dimensionality alteration   24
   extreme situation   23–24
   interactive experiment   24
   pictorial analogy   23
Crocker, Betty   64
Cuban, Mark   *143*
'curse of knowledge'   41
CVS   *34*

da Vinci, Leonardo   35, *35*
Dallas Mavericks   *143*
de la Garza, Sam   46
Dell
   Della   143–44
   Ideastorm   149
Devil's Dictionary, The   30
Dickinson, Emily   7
Dilbert   93
Dion, Celine   *68*
Disney, Walt   172
Domino's Pizza   *67*
   'Boogergate' crisis   141, 142
dopamine   104
Dove   49, *50, 101*
   'Evolution'   *147*
   'Onslaught(er)' parody   *147*, 148
Doyle Dane Bernbach   21
Dragoon, John   *143*
Dreyfuss, Julia Louis   *68*
Driven: How Human Nature Shapes Our Choices   92
Du Plessis, Erik   157, 160, 161
Duke Power   158, 162
Dumont, Margaret   2
Duracell   153
Dutch Lady   128

EDS   153

Effective Advertising: Understanding When, How, and Why Advertising Works   163
Ekman, Paul   62
Electronic Arts   168
emotional markets   94–95, *96, 97*
Emotionomics   83, 147
Energizer   65
Enron   162
E-Trade   113
executive blogging   140–43, *143*
eye tracking   15, 37
   and logo placement   *36*, 37, 56
   and text   17
   and use of faces in advertisements   56

Facebook   118, 151
face-recognition units (FRUs)   60–61
faces, use of   55–70
   and brand personality   55
   casting   65–68, *67, 68*
   celebrities, use of   61, 62, *68*
   close-ups   61
   coldness   68, *69*
   gender   62
   looking away   62
   motion   57, 61
   smiles, true vs social   62–65, *63*, 169
      recognizing the difference   65
   visual processing of faces   *58*
   why faces are used   55–61
      face-recognition units (FRUs)   60–61
      fusiform face area (FFA)   57, *58*
facial coding   2, 3, 11
   and brand loyalty   166
   and casting in advertisements   55
   and engagement   27–29
   and lying   *56*
   and 'message-itis'   40
   and motivators in advertising   93
   and peaks in advertising   81
   and responses to category advertising   *106*
   and types of advertising   *159, 160*

familiarity   45–54
  comfort zone, importance of   *50*,
    50–52
  discomfort with strangers   52–54, *53*
  feedback loop, triggering the   47–48,
    48–49
    casting   48
    music   49
    repetition   48
  why familiarity works   45–47
Fast Company   6
FedEx   *154*
feeling points   28, *28*
Ferrari   110
Fiat   42
Field, Peter   5, 6
Field, Sally   *68*
First Flavor   20
Fiske, Neil   95
Flickr   151
fMRI brain scans   29, *60*, 68, *69*, *105*,
  124
Ford   *34*, 48, *101*
  Ford Fiesta   47
Fortune   33, *34*
Fox   63
Freud, Sigmund   45
fusiform face area (FFA)   57, *58*

Gallup Organization   29
Garfield, Bob   4, 146, 162
Garnier   *101*
Gatorade   98
gender in advertising   143–46
General Mills   17, 64
  'Betty Crocker'   64
General Motors   *34, 101*, 132, 166
  Cadillac Eldorado   21
Gigerenzer, Gerd   30
Gillette   *101*, 167
Gimme!   102
Gladwell, Malcolm   3
Godin, Seth   21
Grandey, Alicia   62
Greenpeace   148
Groundswell   146

*Gut Feelings: The Intelligence of the
  Unconscious*   30

Hallward, John   6, 102
Harley-Davidson   88
Hart, Leslie   51
Haysbert, Dennis   *68*, 134
Healthy Choice   *68*
Heath, Chip and Heath, Dan   41, 126
Heath, Robert   79
*Hero and the Outlaw, The: Building
  Extraordinary Brands Through the
  Power of Archetypes*   100
Hesse, Dan   67
Hey, Whipple, Squeeze This   7, 14, 34
*High Impact: How YOU Can Create
  Advertising That SELLS*   94
Holbrook, Morris   105
Home Depot   *34*
hope, selling   103–20
  behavioural economics   112–17,
    114
    conformity   115
    impulsivity   116
    inequality aversion   116–17
    loss aversion   113
    overconfidence   116
    probability blinders   115–16
    resistance to change   114–15
  and happiness   103–04, *104*
    fear of corruption   107, 108–09
    relationship between happiness and
      hope   108, *108*
    responses to category
      advertising   *106*
    sources of happiness   107
  reciprocity   117–18
Hopkins, Claude   167
How the Brain Works   51
How We Decide   129
Hyundai   *101*

Iacocca, Lee   *67*
IBM   *34*, 115
ICICI Prudential   132
Iezzi, Teressa   144

ING *67*
Institute of Practitioners in
  Advertising 5
Ipsos 6, 50, 134
Irwin, Sam 114

Jensen, Rolf 95
Jesus Jeans 13
Jezebel 99
Jiffy Lube *150*
Jobs, Steve 30, 172
Johnson, Lyndon Baines 56
Jones, John Philip 6–7, 39, 41, 163
Jordan, Michael *68*
Joy, Kevin 135
Jung-Beeman, Mark 104
Jupiter Media *143*
JWT 133

Keep It Simple Stupid (KISS) 27
Kelly, Margaret *67*
Kiley, David 112
Kit Kat 133
Klein, Calvin 13, 14
Klein, Stefan 107
Knutson, Brian 123
Kohler *97*
Kraft 17
Kuhmann, Arkadi *67*

Lance, Steve 89
Land Rover 46
Lange, Dorothea 134
'Last Supper' 35, *35*
Lawrence, Paul 92, 93
Lehrer, Jonah 129
Leo Burnett 76–77, 134
Lever, William Hesketh 6
LG 123
Li, Charlene 146
Lie To Me 3
limbic system *see* brain science
LinkedIn 142
Little Blue Book of Advertising, The 4,
  89, 118
Loewenstein, George 123, 126

logo, placement of 35–37, *36*, *37*, 84,
  85
Lynch, Kevin *143*

Made to Stick 41, 126
Mark, Margaret 100, 101
Marlboro 76–77
Marx, Groucho 2
Mays, Billy 9–12
McCann, Jim *67*
McDonald's 21, *68*, *101*
  McDonald, Ronald 23
McEnroe, John 102
Meckler, Alan *143*
memorable, making it 71–86
  brand recall 83–84
  death, using *74*
  leveraging emotion 76–77
  logo, placement of 84, *85*
  pacing 79–80, *80*
  patience 82
  peaks 80–82, *82*
  retention process 74–75
  'Truth' vs 'Think' campaigns 72–74,
    76–77, *78*
    quiz 72–73
    why 'Truth' won 76–77
Mentos 148
Mercedes Benz 14, 42
'message-itis' 40–41
Microsoft 54
Miller Beer 16, 146
  Miller High Life 115
Millward Brown 157
Mobil 75
Mona Lisa 57, *59*
Monster 115
Motrin 146
MSNBC 63
MySpace 151

narrative advertising 158, 159, 163–64,
  165
Nast, Thomas 75
National Car Rental 46, 102
NBC 63

neo-cortex   *see* brain science
Nestlé
  Kit Kat   133
Neutrogena   *101*
New Belgium Beer   *150*
New Yorker   88
Newmark, Craig   *143*
Nike   23
Nirvana   51
Nohria, Nitin   92, 93
Novell   *143*

Obama, Barack   112
Ogilvy on Advertising   31
Ogilvy, David   31
Olay   *101*
Olive Garden   *147*
Omnicom Group   4
One Show, The   23
'on-emotion', meaning of   1–2
'on-message', being   1, 2, *3*, 4, 89, *90*,
  113, 141, 169
Ortony, Andrew   93
Orwell, George   62
Outdoor Advertising Association of
  America   40

parody commercials   146–48, *147*
Pearson, Carol   100, 101
Peel 'n' Taste Strips   20
Pepsi   *68*, 112
persuasion, creating   164–69
  casting   169
  consistency   168–69
  fairness vs desire   166–68
  familiarity   166
Peugeot   42
Pew Internet & American Life
  Project   147
Philip Morris   74, 76, 77
  Marlboro Man   76–77
  'Think' campaign   74, 76
Philipps, Sam   141
Pirro Brothers   90–92, *91*
Plutchik, Robert   98
Politico   63

Popeye's   58
*Positioning: The Battle for Your
  Mind*   51, 87, 103
PowerPoint®   35
price sensitivity   6
price, leading with   121–35
  alternative strategies
    brand associations   133–34
    co-creation   134
    sensory route   132–33
  and brand integrity   131–32
  and brand loyalty   130–31, *131*
  and inviting contempt   127–28
  and decision making   128–30
  and engagement   126–27
  and hope   123–25, *124*
  internet price comparison   122
  problems with   *122*, 122–32
  and surprise   123
Pringle, Hamish   5, 6
Procter & Gamble   149
  'Tide to Go'   98
Progressive Insurance   167, 168
'prosumers'   140, 147, 148
PSE&G   19

Quiksilver   *18*

Realogy Corporation   134, 141
relevancy   87–102
  brand personality types   100–02, *101*
  emotional markets   94–95, *96, 97*
  identifying with emotions   97–100,
    99
  motivations   89–94, *90*
    motivational categories   93, *93*
  and product/service categories   88
  and social media   *88*
  what's in it for me? (WIIFM)   87–89
Remax Realty   *67*
Return Path   *143*
Reynolds Wrap   153
Rich, Joe   19
Ries, Al   7, 51, 87, 103
Ries, Laura   7
right-left brain specialization   33, 59

Rosetta Stone   17
Rotten, Johnny   172

Salangane   116
Sam's Club   134
Santa Claus   75
Save the Children   126
Schwarz, Jonathan   *143*
Science of Happiness, The   107
Scientific Advertising   167
Scruton, Roger   57
Seattle's Best   17
Seligman, Marty   107
senses, engaging the   9–25
    creative templates
        competition   24
        consequences   23
        dimensionality alteration   24
        extreme situation   23–24
        interactive experiment   24
        pictorial analogy   23
    sensory contrasts   20–21, 22–23
    smell   19
    stopping power   9, 10
    taste   20
    touch   20
    visual input   13–17
        guidelines for imagery   *15*, 15–17,
            16
        and literacy   14
    voice and sounds   10–12
serotonin   104
Shakespeare, William   38–39
Shields, Brooke   13, *13*, 14
Shiffman, Denise   7, 131
Silverstein, Michael   95
Simon, Herbert   41
simplicity
    engagement   27–30
        feeling points   28, *28*
    frustration, overcoming   30–38, *31*
        accessibility   32
        editing speed   38
        hierarchy of visuals   34–35, *35*
        logo, placement of   35–37, *36*, *37*
        perspective   32–34

voice-overs   29, 30
words, use of   38–42
    'message-itis'   40–41
    pain-gain contrasts   39–40
    word length   41–42
Simpsons, The   113
Slovic, Paul   126
Small Is the New Big   21
Small, Deborah   126
Smells Like Teen Spirit   51
smiles, true vs social   62–65, *63*, 169
    recognizing the difference   65
Snoop Dogg   67
Snuggie   *147*, 148
social media   4, *88*, 118, 137, 140
    Domino's Pizza   141
    Ford Fiesta   47
    Land Rover Twitter campaign   46
    see also executive blogging;
        Facebook; Flickr; LinkedIn;
        MySpace; parody commercials;
        Twitter; YouTube
Song of the Open Road   111
Sony
    PlayStation® 2   20
Sopranos, The   53
Sprint   *67*
Star Trek   113
Starbucks   *101*
Stein, Gertrude   132
Stuart, Greg   6, 30, 83, 92–93
Suarez, Ben   41
Subway   *101*
Sullivan, Luke   7, 14, 34, 88
Sun   141
Sun Microsystems   *143*
Sundar, Mario   142, 143
Sunset Boulevard   61
Swanson, Gloria   61

Tellis, Gerard   163–64
testimonials   157–58, 162–63
The Dream Society   95
The Sex Pistols   172
Third Wave, The   140
Three Dog Night   40

Tobii   15
Toffler, Alvin   140, 147
Tourism Queensland   125
Toyota   *101*
Transavia   117
Tripoldi, Joe   112
TriStar Auto Care study   154, *155*
Trout, Jack   51, 87, 103
TWBA/Chiat/Day   6
Twitter   46, 118, 140, 151

Unilever   *50*
   and social media   148
   Suave   168
USADREVIEW   23

value advertising   *see* price, leading
   with
values, mirroring   137–52
   cause marketing   149–51, *150*
   change in world economies   *138*,
      138–39
   executive blogging   140–43, *143*
   gender portrayals   143–46
   parody commercials   146–48, *147*
   shifts in consumer expectations   *139*,
      139–40
van Gogh, Vincent   172
Verizon   *34*
Virgin Records   172
Volkswagen   42
   'Think Small'   21, *22*, 23

Wallace, George   31
Walmart   *34*, *104*, 127
Wannamaker, John   6
Watergate   114
web design   33–34, *34*
We Gotta Get Out of This Place (If It's
   the Last Thing We Ever Do)   *110*
What Sticks: Why Most Advertising
   Fails and How to Guarantee Yours
   Succeeds   6, 92
what's in it for me? (WIIFM)   87–89
Whitman, Walt   111
Wilde, Oscar   116
Wilder, Gene   20
Willy Wonka and the Chocolate
   Factory   20
Witt, Gary   94
Woll, Jeff   89
word of mouth   118, 156
World of Warcraft   *147*
Wrigley's   133
'Writing the Codes on Blogs'   141
Wundt, William   45
   Wundt's curve   45, 79, 172

Young, Charles   83
YouTube   10, 134, 141, 146, 147, 151

Zajonc, Robert   47